A Grafted Tree

*A Memoir of Adoption, Disability,
Identity, and Family*

Kathleen Tumminello

Copyright © 2023 Kathleen Tumminello All rights reserved.

No part of this book may be reproduced, or stored in a retrieval system, or transmitted in any form or by any means, electronic, mechanical, photocopying, recording, or otherwise, without express written permission of the publisher.

Cover design by: watchusglow.com
Author Photo: Courtesy of Moses Farrow Photography
Printed in the United States of America

Author's Note

Nature vs. nurture—the age-old conundrum. What makes us who we are? It's both, you might say. I agree, but when I set out to write this memoir about raising an adopted child with disabilities, I found that nature played a far larger role than I expected. I also discovered that this story is not about adoption, disabilities, or even raising children. It's about accepting one another for who we are and understanding and valuing our differences and identities.

I'm hoping, dear reader, that with all the divisive societal issues and movements swirling around us these days, you can see some parallels in my small story—perhaps even to plant some of your own seeds of hopefulness in this beautiful, imperfect world.

Fall 1979

You would think I'd remember every detail of that day, but my memory can only dispense fragments; a kitchen corner where the wall phone hung, a scrap of paper, some scribbled words, a simple question, and a pitiful image in my mind. So, I suppose that's where the story begins.

I had just hung up the phone and was looking at the words I had jotted down while trying to listen to everything that I had been told:

malnourished
failure to thrive
burns lower body
doesn't speak
head shaved
about 2-3 years old
can't leave behind
beautiful

All words written in pencil…as if they could be erased.

I held that scrap of paper with those unsettling words and gazed out the kitchen window. It was a beautiful fall day. I needed to think. Looking at the trees and the patches of sunshine on grass beneath them put me in a calmer state of mind. Sunny days made me feel optimistic, upbeat, and happy, but this was different…I couldn't be deceived by the sun. Did I stand there for one minute? Ten? Twenty? I don't know. I only remember not wanting to call Jack. I wanted to be alone with my thoughts first. The clear day had morphed. It became mist-laden, and through the gauzy vapor an image had emerged—a baby—burned, abandoned, and languishing. The image kept trying to overwhelm my thought process. Fighting through the haze, I returned to what Jean, our adoption caseworker, had just told me. "I know you and Jack were hoping for a healthy infant, but I thought you might be interested. This is a special case." It *was* a special case, but what about my career? I was a newly registered nurse, an RN just getting started with hospital nursing. But this baby…that image…I turned away from the window and picked up the phone.

"Jack? They found a little girl for us."

"That's fantastic! How old is she? What did Jean say?"

"She said her friend, Connie Boll, who's a social worker, was in Seoul looking for a baby for a client. She found a little boy, but then came across a little girl with burns." With a shaky hand, I picked up the piece of paper and quickly told Jack what I remembered. I took a deep breath and paused. "The problem is Connie thinks the little girl is a failure-to-thrive baby and doesn't want to leave her behind."

"What's failure to thrive?"

"Well, when babies don't get enough attention or care, some give up. They become passive and stop learning how to do all the usual things babies do—you know, like sitting up, crawling, and walking."

"So how serious is this?"

"If no intervention occurs…the baby can die. That's why Connie's so concerned." There was silence on the other end of the phone. I couldn't see Jack's face to judge any reaction he was having. So, winding and unwinding the phone cord around my finger, I continued telling him what I had pieced together from my conversation with Jean.

"Jean told me that Connie had suffered from burns on her neck as a child, and that was one reason she was drawn to the baby. She said the baby is beautiful, and she's developing a bond with her."

Still silence on Jack's end.

"Oh, and Jean also said the little girl seemed to have a fear of men, and it might take a while for her to warm up to you."

It was a lot of information for us both to process. The moment had come: me in the corner of a sunny kitchen, and Jack at his office desk. Did we want this child? Matthew, our eleven-year-old, was in middle school and doing well. He had a gentleness about him and knew we were waiting for another baby. However, Jason, our four-year-old, also adopted from Korea, was a handful. His hyperactivity kept us both entertained and challenged. So, the question remained: Did we want this child? Could we do this?

After a long pause, Jack asked one question. "Does she make eye contact?"

"Yes," I said.

"Well, that's good enough for me," he replied.

I don't remember a single second of the rest of that day.

Unfamiliar Surroundings

Talking to one of my friends about our decision to adopt this baby, she said to me, "Of all the friends in our group, if anyone would do something like this, it would be the two of you." New adventures and discoveries invigorated Jack and me. It's what had attracted us to each other. For instance, I remember the time in 1972: We were young, twenty-four and twenty-six years old. Jack had just finished teaching a week-long computer programming course in Paris, so with an extra week to ourselves, and armed with a Michelin map and travel guide, the three of us, Jack, Matthew, and I, were exploring the French countryside. Our little rented Peugeot was lurching up a narrow, curving street in a small town outside Paris. "Okay, now take your foot off the brake and let the clutch out slowly while stepping on the gas. Not that slow! Give it more gas!" Three-year-old Matthew was in the back seat surrounded by swaying luggage. I was teaching Jack how to drive a stick-shift car that was about to stall on a steep section of the cobblestone street.

That had been an adventure. But this sobering decision was not about some momentary escapade. It was a child's life. It was permanent, and we knew full well there was no road map that could guide us.

Our wanderlust turned inward while waiting for this baby. There were so many unknowns to be discovered. Connie had arranged for the toddlers—the little girl and the little boy to be placed with a Baptist minister and his wife, Harold and Audrey Gateley, while the paperwork was being completed. The little girl, who was named Doo Hee, and the little boy were not siblings, but both had been abandoned and had spent months "warehoused" in Seoul Children's Hospital. Doo Hee was recovering from burns, and the little boy had cerebral palsy. Through correspondence with our social worker, we learned that Connie's client was the actress Mia Farrow, and she had named the little boy Misha.

Audrey would send us letters (via Connie) of her observations of Doo Hee with redacted sections where she mentioned Misha. She also sent pictures of Melissa (the name Jack and I were giving her), who was now gaining weight, and one touching black-and-white picture of the two toddlers sitting on her bed. They were wearing overalls and were in stockinged feet. Misha had his right arm around Melissa's shoulder, and she was leaning in to kiss him on his cheek.

Maybe it was because of the redactions in Audrey's letters, but Jack and I had never attempted to contact Mia Farrow. We felt it important to respect her family's privacy. Besides, our focus needed to be on Melissa since Audrey's letters gave us a picture of a very fragile toddler.

These are some excerpts from Audrey's letters:

11/29/1979

"She hasn't said one word, not even the babbling sounds, but she laughs and squeals when she is delighted about something.

When she cries, she holds it in for a while and the tears roll but her lips are closed and no sound comes out and then finally she lets go and cries. I think she has probably been told not to cry and scolded for crying."

12/26/1979

"…when she cries, she holds her breath and really goes into an emotional production. She doesn't cry often, and sometimes doesn't make a production of it. I talked to a friend of mine about her. She is a counselor and majored in child guidance. She said Doo Hee does that because she's been ignored so long and that her crying never produced any end (regarding whatever she was frustrated about at the time), and so she gradually began to carry the crying further. My friend says it will take a long time to heal her emotionally, and of course TLC is the answer! We also feel that possibly she has been physically abused at some point since she can't stand to be surprised. She startles easily and she goes into a crying fit if she sees anyone "play-wrestling" or "horsing around". She also cannot stand anything that she interprets as rejection, absolutely no harsh scolding! Of course she doesn't need scolding anyway, she's a very sweet little girl and happy most of the time."

Her Korean documentation had her just shy of four years old. Harold Gateley wrote in a letter dated January 30, 1980:

"They (Seoul Children's Hospital) arbitrarily gave her a birthdate of March 12, 1976. It seems to us that she is at least a year younger than this…"

In one letter, Audrey described a small growth on Melissa's chest that appeared to be growing larger. It had been there when she had first come to them, but Audrey was concerned. She went to the Seoul Welfare Society (SWS, the agency responsible for the children, akin to our Office of Child Welfare) to see if there was any note of the growth in her medical records. There was nothing there. The SWS doctor looked at it and thought it was okay but told her to have a doctor look at it again if it continued to grow. It was becoming larger, but there was nothing we could do from such a distance.

February 12, 1980. The day finally arrived, and just as we had for Jason, we drove to New York and waited at the same arrival gate at JFK for our new baby. While Jason busied himself crawling over and under the rows of blue Naugahyde molded seats, Jack, Matthew, and I craned our necks trying to spot the Gateleys in the throng of passengers fanning out from the airline gate. "It's them," I said. A middle-aged woman was carrying a little almond-eyed baby with short black hair in a green toddler outfit, and a taller, sandy-haired man was by her side.

Melissa looked dazed and frightened, and I was trying very hard not to cry—that was the last thing she needed to experience. Jack was watching me warily since I had had an extreme emotional reaction and then dissolved into a sobbing mess when Jason had arrived five years earlier. Audrey placed Melissa in my arms. I can't remember what we said, but I'm sure we mumbled something about our sincere gratitude and thanks. It was a brief exchange, and looking back, I think Audrey and Harold had been trying to hold their emotions in check, too. They had been foster parents to many children and probably knew it was best not to linger during these sensitive moments.

It was a fifteen-hour flight from Seoul, and Audrey said that Melissa had been sick with motion sickness for most of it. Since it was late in the evening, we checked into a motel in Connecticut, near Jack's parents' home. I carried Melissa into the motel room and placed her on the bed. She was dry-eyed, and the only observable outward emotion was a look of sadness and fear. It was similar to the look Jason had had when he arrived at six months of age—wide-eyed and continually looking around. It breaks your heart. Everything is unfamiliar. New sounds, smells, surroundings, language, and, maybe most frightening... *Who are these people? And who are you, dear baby?* I thought.

I unwrapped Melissa from the clothes she had come in; a pair of little "puppy" slip-on sneakers, a kelly green toddler outfit with a white-and-red embroidered bib top, and underneath that outfit, a little cotton pajama set. Carefully taking off the pajamas, we got our first glimpse of her extensive burns and that growth on her chest that Jack and I were worried about. It was a shocking sight for Jack and the boys. Their silence, especially Jason's—the boy of 1,000 questions—confirmed my thoughts. How much pain had she endured? It was disturbing to see, so I tried to box in those feelings and went into nursing assessment mode—clinical and objective. I had to be the nurse at that moment and not the mother. I could see that the scarring from her burns was still fresh and deep pink. She was burned from her buttocks to the soles of her feet. There was a large, thick keloid growth on her right thigh and tight adhesions behind her knees, preventing her from easily extending her legs. It would all need surgery, but that would have to be at a later date. As a nurse, I also knew that burns on 20 percent of an infant or a young child's body are very serious and potentially life-threatening. Judging from what I could see (using the quick, visual medical "rule of nines" to estimate burn size), Melissa's burns covered approximately 15 percent of her body. And since we knew Melissa had been found on the street approximately eleven months earlier, with open burn wounds vulnerable to infection, it was a wonder she had even survived. The growth on her chest, just above her left nipple, was a strange pea-sized nodule with a depression in the middle. It didn't look like anything I recognized from my nursing training, but I already had an appointment scheduled with our pediatrician.

While I undressed her and changed her diaper, Melissa remained passive, silent, and wide-eyed. Jack stayed in the background getting the boys settled while I got Melissa to eat some oatmeal, thanks to Jack and Matthew's late-night run to Howard Johnson's. We had brought two new toys with us: a plastic ball with cutouts of various shapes and a little soft doll. Melissa showed no interest in the ball at all, but when she saw the doll, she became upset and instantly flung it across the bed—much to Jason's amusement and our surprise. Forgetting about Jean's "fearful of men" comment, Jack instinctively picked Melissa up. For the next several hours, he had to walk around the motel room holding her since she would tighten her lips in a pouting manner, like she was trying not to cry, and tightly hug his neck if he tried to put her down or give her to anyone. Jack got some respite when he discovered he could stand Melissa on the bathroom counter, and she could kiss her reflection in the mirror. Abandonment can be a huge issue with some adopted children. And Melissa, who had been abandoned on the street and then left in a children's home for months with little attention, had internalized this and seemed to be telling us—no, *YELLING* at us, "Hey, don't ever leave me!"

Midnight approached, and Melissa seemed to be feeling better. There was a little color in her cheeks (or so my clinical nurse's observation told me) and no vomiting. The boys were still awake, and we all just wanted to get home. "Let's go," Jack said.

"I'll have to hold her," I said. "She's not going to let me put her in the car seat." The ride home to Massachusetts was quiet. The boys fell asleep, but Melissa, ever vigilant to her surroundings, clung to me while Jack drove.

Finally, we were home. Melissa had fallen asleep, and I gently placed her in the crib in our bedroom. It had been an exhausting day for all of us. Waking up the following morning, I saw her standing in her crib, pointing to the floor. She wanted to get out. How long had she been standing there? There had been no crying, not even a tiny sound. She looked so sad and had an empty, far-off look on her face, as if she wasn't expecting anything to happen. I jumped out of bed and picked her up. "It's going to be okay, baby girl," I whispered. "It's going to be okay."

Reception

After we married, we spent a year in Binghamton, New York, while Jack went to graduate school. Matthew was born the following August, 1968. A beautiful six-pound, eight-ounce baby boy who looked just like his dad. With two-week-old Matthew in tow, we moved to Jack's hometown of Stamford, Connecticut, where Jack got his first "real" job. But I missed my family terribly. Having a new baby, little money, no car, and few chances to meet new friends, I felt overwhelmed and isolated. Moreover, while I'm sure Jack's parents loved their son and new grandchild, I found them distant and cold.

It was hard for me to relate to a family like that. They probably had a hard time adjusting to me as well. Jack had an older sister and brother, yet he had been the first to get married. In old-fashioned Italian families such as the one Jack's father was trying to hold on to, usually the oldest daughter gets married, then the oldest son. And here I come, a small, timid, young, Irish woman—barely twenty, and looking like a sixteen-year-old—marrying their youngest son. It wasn't the way it was supposed to be done.

I always found my father-in-law's old-world view of family—*Sicilian* family, *his* family, ironic. He had married a tall, fair-skinned Polish girl who came from a large, happy family in Upstate New York, but he had paid the price for this transgression: His mother had never considered his wife part of the family. As in many Italian families, the matriarch is in charge of *la famiglia,* and my father-in-law's mother was no exception. She was all of four foot ten, spoke only a few words of English, dressed in widow black, and was a brute. By the time I entered the picture, Jack's father was still cowering, trying to placate her. He would jump up from his chair and rush to the phone whenever his mother called. I'd watch as his demeanor would abruptly change. He'd turn toward the wall, cup the mouthpiece with his hand, and in a lowered voice he'd talk to her in Italian. The few words he spoke in English, "Ma…no, no… okay! Yes, Ma…yes, okay, Ma, no…" left no doubt that he was being given a piece of her mind.

After a year in Stamford, we moved to Massachusetts, and three years later, bought our first home not far from Chelmsford. It was during this period that Jack and I found out we were unable to have any more children. Turning to adoption, we attended a prospective parents' meeting at a nearby adoption agency. But since we already had a biological child, and the wait list for Caucasian babies was limited to childless couples, our only option was either an older child or a baby from another country. International adoptions in the early seventies were mostly from Korea. Korean intercountry adoption had begun in 1956, due largely to the efforts of Henry and Bertha Holt, evangelists who had founded the Holt Adoption Agency to respond to the thousands of abandoned Korean War orphans, many of whom had been fathered by American servicemen.

We had left Matthew at my parents' so we could go to the meeting. But during the ride back, Jack had remained quiet.

Parking our car in their driveway, Jack shut the engine off and sat staring ahead and said, "I don't know."

"What do you mean?" I said.

"I don't think I can do this."

"Why? Because the babies are from Korea?"

"No, of course not."

"Don't you want another baby?"

"Yes…but…I don't think I can love an adopted baby as much as I love Matthew."

I stared at his face for a moment and then put my head on his chest and cried bitterly into his shirt. I couldn't ask this of him. It would be unfair to him and the baby. There was nothing more to say. A few weeks after that discussion, Jack told me he had changed his mind about adopting.

"Why?" I asked.

"Because I saw how devastated you were when I told you I was afraid that I couldn't love an adopted baby as much as Matthew."

I was so clouded by an acute maternal longing for another baby that I never considered the fact that he was giving in to *my* desire while his fear remained.

Jack's mother already knew about our decision to adopt a baby from Korea, but approaching her husband about it was not something she wanted to do, so we drove to Connecticut for the weekend to help break the news to his father.

Matthew, Jack's mother, and I and were in the kitchen when the argument erupted. Jack had gone into the living room to broach the subject with his father, and within seconds, I heard his father's deep, loud, guttural voice erupt with rage.

"What the hell are you talking about! What kind of goddamn *stupid* idea is that! You don't know what the hell you're doing…!" And it continued in that vein.

For Jack and his mother, arguments of this sort were all too familiar. But I froze in place at the kitchen table. I shot a quick glance at Jack's mother, who was standing next to the stove as she turned away from us and focused her attention on something on the counter. I felt an unpleasant warmth in my face and neck and a tightness in my stomach. Matthew, age five, had stopped eating his lunch; he looked up at me with frightened eyes. I could barely breathe. Neither Matthew nor I was used to emotional outbursts like this one. I put my arm around his shoulder and before I could do anything more, I heard Jack say, "Well, that's what we're going to do, Dad."

"Then don't come back here if you do!" his father shot back.

Jack barked, "That's fine, we'll stay away but understand; this is *my* family, *our* decision, and *you* will not bother *us*!"

Jack came around to the kitchen doorway, with his face strained, and looked at Matthew and me.

"C'mon we have to leave."

We quickly gathered our belongings and said goodbye to his mother.

I was proud of Jack. He'd never stood up to his father's bullying while growing up. It was easier to "just keep the peace," as his mother would say, but this time, this time when it mattered most, he had spoken up and defended *his* family. On the quiet ride home, Jack said, "You know, I don't think he really meant what he said." I wasn't so sure. I didn't answer. I was upset. But after some time, I realized we had just blown up this man's already-frayed image of his quasi-Italian family's identity. Having been brought up by a controlling, stern mother in an unhappy Sicilian family, he was suspicious of outsiders and ever vigilant about his family's appearance to others, lest he be judged as an inadequate father and provider.

Jack told me a story about the time he and his brother had set up a lemonade stand in their driveway next to the sidewalk. Jack's father had come home from work, spotted the stand, jumped out of his truck, and in a frenzy of profanity-laced rage, kicked over the table, then stormed up the stairs and into the kitchen, screaming at his wife.

"What kind of a f…ing, goddamned woman are you! You let them do this! What? You don't think I can provide for my goddamn family?!"

Appearances to him were all wrapped up in Italian family honor, pride, and identity. Our next child would not be a continuation of *la famiglia* bloodline. We had set up our lemonade stand, and he was powerless to overturn it.

Jack's father was too proud to admit he was sorry or wrong, so the best course of action, Jack thought, was to act as if it never had happened. Two years later, when we finally got the call about Jason's arrival date, Jack called home and spoke to his mother. He told her we were picking Jason up at JFK in a couple of days and would like to stay overnight since Jason would arrive late in the evening. She said we could, and I never learned if she had told my father-in-law.

I thought I was handling the excitement of picking up our new baby pretty well, but on our way to the airport, I felt a wave of nausea overtake me. We had waited so long for this day, and it didn't help that we got caught in a rush-hour traffic snarl with Jack announcing that we would be late. How could we be late for Jason's arrival!

Jack tells me that we got to the airport late. But we were okay, because there had been a flight delay. I say, Jack "*tells me*," because I have no memory of time that night. As I write this now, I am astonished that I didn't know we had had a five-hour delay.

I don't like to show my emotions in public, and that night, they were fifteen on a scale of one to ten. Thinking we were late, I was half-running through the terminal and breathing hard, when I saw the sign for the Pan Am lounge just ahead. As we turned the corner to enter, I saw in front of me "hundreds" of people. (Jack kindly tells me now that there were about fifty people in the lounge.) Parents-to-be, friends, and relatives—all waiting for the babies. I burst into tears and buried my head in Jack's chest. "I can't go in there! There are too many people! It's too much! I can't do this!"

We backed up around the corner for me to calm down for a few minutes, but then Jack took my arm and gently coaxed me into the lounge. "We have to go in there," he whispered. I'm assuming Matthew followed us. I desperately needed a diversion to keep my mind and emotions from exploding. Mindless talk about the weather—anything except babies. Then, a tall, kind-looking man approached me. I'm guessing he saw how distressed I appeared and tried to help. He bent down and extended his hand. In it was the picture of his soon-to-be adopted baby. Everyone had their photo. It's all you look at in the months running up to actually holding the baby in your arms. *No, no. No pictures!* I turned away from the gentleman holding his photo, sat down, and stared at the wall. I thought if I just focused on the vertical, blue, and silver metallic stripes of the wallpaper, I could keep my emotions in check, which I did with spectacular results: I put myself in a semi-catatonic state. That is all I remember of what Jack says was the next five hours. I should have dissolved into a sobbing, choking, nose-running, embarrassing display. Ten minutes of slobbering would have done the trick. My behavior mortified poor Jack, but he said he understood what happened.

I emerged from my self-induced stupor when I heard someone saying the plane had arrived, and they wanted only the parents to go to the gate. *Get me out of this room with all these people. I could handle that*, I thought. We left Matthew in the lounge area, with the remaining family members and friends. While waiting for the babies to exit the plane with their escorts, I sat between Jack and a woman who appeared older than me. She reached over and patted my hand. "You're going to be fine, dear."

I could allow myself to be vulnerable now, and so the tears flowed when I held Jason in my arms. "He's beautiful, he's beautiful," I kept saying or rather, crying while carrying him back to the lounge area. Matthew was jumping up and down and waving to us across the room. He had set out a diaper-changing mat, a clean diaper, and a bottle of formula for his new baby brother.

Pulling into his parents' driveway, Jack said, "Let me carry him in." I understood what he was doing. A happy, but sleepy, seven-year-old Matthew trailed behind. Proudly, defiantly, and without saying a word, Jack walked into his parents' living room with Jason in the crook of his arm and handed his father a fuzzy-haired little six-month-old baby. His father looked stunned. He quickly put Jason down on the couch, but I thought I detected a very faint smile on his face, or maybe it was the lack of anger in his face I mistook for a smile. I really didn't care, as long as there were no outbursts from him.

It was approaching midnight, and since there was a good deal of tension in our visit, we were glad to close the bedroom door. Jack, Matthew, and I piled onto the bed with Jason in the middle of the heap. Jack propped him up on his knees so we all could see him. Jason made a cute baby noise and Jack got him to repeat it. The squint of his eyes, the broad smile, the laughter, the *glow* of Jack's face told me everything I needed to know about his fear of not loving this baby as much as Matthew. We left early the next morning, eager to get back to Massachusetts. First stop—my parents' home.

The Compound

Babies were big deals in my family. With each new baby—my sister's three and our Matthew—my father would proclaim, "This one's the cutest and smartest baby ever." He'd say that until the next one arrived. It was one thing Jack loved about my family. Babies in our family got a lot of attention, especially from Dad. Every grandchild got to sit on his lap while each one "helped" him dunk his toast or doughnut into his Saturday morning coffee. He got such a kick out of that. I even have memories of doing the same when I was a child. So, of course, when Jason came, "He was the cutest." But perhaps because Jason was the first Asian baby my father was ever exposed to, Dad couldn't get enough of him. He even stopped by our home after Jason arrived, pulled a chair up next to the crib, and sat there watching him until he woke from his nap.

My parents had a comfortable old house in Chelmsford, Massachusetts. It was where I had grown up from the age of ten until the day Jack and I had married. In fact, our wedding reception had been held in the backyard. About a year after Jason arrived, my parents gave us some land behind their house to build our dream home. Their white clapboard one-hundred-year-old house was in an established, older neighborhood on one of the original streets in town. It sat on three acres of land that was dotted with a number of apple trees—vestiges of an old apple orchard. The house had a generous front yard, well off the road. The woman who had lived in the house before my parents had bought it had been an avid gardener. As a result, the lower acre-and-a-half—where my parents' home was situated—was populated with aging, somewhat neglected, but still glorious perennial flower beds, an assortment of grass paths, hedges, enclaves of hemlock trees, arbors with roses, flowering vines, stone walls, and a scattering of little, hidden nooks of plantings and trees. In my ten-year-old girl's imagination, it had been an enchanted playground. There was even a space that I considered a "secret room." It was located on the edge of the cultivated part of the yard; the other half beyond was a field of grass and apple trees. To get to it, you had to walk up a grass path between flower beds, and past a small, shaded pool made of large pieces of natural stone that was near the base of three mature hemlock trees. Beyond the trees was a rose-covered arbor that opened to my "room." It was a sunny patch of grass about twelve feet square, bordered by spirea bushes, which, when in bloom, softly arched downward from the weight of prolific white blossoms. Opposite the arbor was a small white gate, which opened to reveal an old, rustic stone fireplace. We built our home on the rise of land just beyond the stone fireplace—my childhood backyard, where Jack had proposed to me. Jack had spent months designing the house. When finished, the two houses became a small compound. Because we didn't have a driveway while the house was being built, and for almost a year afterward, we parked our car in my parents' driveway and walked up through a path—a botanical umbilical cord—between the homes.

The extended family was confusing to outsiders, but it was our family. My sister's husband had died a few years earlier, and she, her new husband, and her youngest child, Erin, from her first husband, were living with my parents. Erin was only a year older than Matthew, but what made it remarkable was the fact that my sister was sixteen years older than me. We never could have imagined we would have children so close in age. The two cousins—Matthew and Erin—were growing up like brother and sister. The compound was a perfect place for multiple adults to watch and nurture these children. We moved into our new house when Matthew was in third grade, and Jason was twenty-one months old. And now, Melissa was waking up in this home. Another baby had arrived at the compound.

Jack was holding Melissa when my family came up to meet our silent, frightened little toddler. I watched Melissa's head turn and eyes widen as she tightened her grip around Jack's neck. From her perspective, it must have been terrifying. Almost every time new adults came into her life, it usually meant something big would happen, and she probably wouldn't like it, a separation, physical pain, or simply strange new occurrences.

Six foot three, with hands that could palm a basketball, and with a warmth that invited you into his orb, Jack was becoming Melissa's go-to protector. He was like a giant "hug machine." Melissa seemed to sense a safety in him. Erin, at thirteen, thought she had a new little cousin to play with and was eager to hold her, but Melissa looked away and bore her face into Jack's neck. It was a while before she would let anyone else hold her. When my sister Pat—the family worrier—got her chance, she saw the burns on Melissa's lower legs, shot me a soulful glance, and handed Melissa to Mom. Mom was the loving, no-nonsense, take-charge, head of the family. She was the one who, when I had become seriously ill the first year of our marriage, had decided she needed to bring me home for medical care. She drove for six hours, alone, at night, fighting rain and thick fog through the Catskills, with only the taillights of tractor-trailers helping her stay on the treacherous mountain roads.

Breaking the melodrama of the moment, Dad made his usual "cutest baby" proclamation. This, of course, was what we all expected him to say, but maybe because of his age—he was sixty-nine—and the fact that he had retired, Dad had developed a special bond with four-year-old Jason that none of the other grandchildren ever had. Jason had almond eyes; a round, little face; an impish smile; and fine, silky black hair that when the sun shone on his head, it looked as if there were a halo shining on his hair. (Our neighbors pointed this out to us when they watched him run through their field.) *Really, a halo on Jason?* He was cute and mischievous, and the mischievous part is what my father loved the most. Unlike Matthew, Jason loved workbenches, tools, cars, trucks, and tractors, and Dad loved them too. He had two red tractors. And when Jason was about two years old, Dad would take the one with the wide seat out of the garage, and with one arm encircling him, would drive around the two properties until "the little guy" fell asleep, dropping him off with my mother, sister, or me, depending on who was in charge. But Melissa was the new grandchild now, and Dad would have to wait before there would be any tractor rides.

Jack spent the better part of the next two days holding Melissa. Nap time meant they would both fall asleep in the easy chair in the family room with Melissa resting on Jack's broad chest. Watching the sleeping pair made me think of when Dad rode Jason to sleep. Even though Dad would have to bide his time with Melissa, she had already captured his heart. Searching for something in my parents' basement months later, I discovered he had written all the names and birthdates of the grandchildren on a cabinet next to his workbench. After Melissa's name, he had no birthdate but wrote "my Valentine, Feb 13"—the day he had first seen her.

A Pooled Teardrop

Daily life changed for our family. Melissa's emotional fragility demanded everyone's attention and vigilance (I had given up my job at the hospital to give her the extra attention she needed, while staying active with occasional per diem work). I knew that extreme stress and/or trauma could cause a non-epileptic seizure, so we tried to do everything possible to mitigate her distress. She did not want to be alone at bedtime, so Jack, Matthew, and I took turns staying with her until she fell asleep. Lying in her crib, she would watch us warily. We, in turn, watched *her* carefully, since Audrey had described an episode we did not want to have repeated.

"Doo Hee had a breath-holding spell last evening when I put her to bed. She was holding back the tears, and when I picked her up, she looked like she was having a mild seizure. It only lasted a second or two, but her eyes rolled and her arms kind of jerked and then it was over. I let her stay up another hour, and then when I put her to bed, she went right to sleep and didn't cry."

During the day, Melissa was always by somebody's side, never venturing away by more than a few feet. She took her naps in a portable crib next to the kitchen and family room so she could see me. Jason was far too busy with his Legos, toy cars, and "adventures" to be all that interested in his new little sister, who was getting all the attention. But Matthew bonded with Melissa immediately, and she with him. He was twelve, tall and slim, and when I watched him pick her up and carry her around the house, it seemed that he could see in Melissa's eyes a mute sadness that called out to him. Looking back, I think Matthew knew that sadness. And when she put her head down on his shoulder, it was as if he was saying, *I know, baby sister, I know.*

I brought Melissa to our pediatrician the week after her arrival. Her physical appearance had changed markedly since she had left the Seoul Children's Hospital. Compared to the gaunt face and shaved head in her passport picture, her face was rounder, and her hair was growing back pixie-style. She looked more and more like a toddler with some baby fat in her face and tummy. In the examining room, I removed the eighteen-month-old-size outfit she was wearing, loosened her diaper, and held her while waiting for the doctor to come in. The doctor knew a little about her condition before he entered the room, but he still couldn't hide a faint wince when he looked at her burns. He wasn't sure what the growth on her chest was (not what I wanted to hear) so he scheduled an appointment with the surgeon and recommended a consult at Shriners Burn Hospital for Children, in Boston.

Throughout the exam, Melissa was silent, but when I put her diaper and clothes back on, she started crying. Hearing her cry as he was leaving the room, the doctor pivoted, patted Melissa on the back, and said, "Don't cry, Missy, don't cry," (we were calling her Missy as a nickname), but she tightened her lips and held her breath.

"Shh, shh, it's okay, it's okay," I murmured as I rocked her up and down to get her to breathe. "She gets even more upset if you say, 'Don't cry,'" I explained. "We think she might have been punished for crying in the children's facility in Korea, so we're teaching her it's *okay* to cry." Crying was something Melissa tried to avoid at all costs, even if it meant holding her breath. It was extreme, and you couldn't convince me she hadn't suffered in the past for crying. I thought she must not have been just ignored, but also physically hurt for doing it.

"She's not going to struggle," I told the surgeon, as I watched the nurse put the papoose-like, Velcro-strapped enclosure on the gurney. I placed Melissa in the center. She didn't move. She lay there passively as they fastened the straps around her small body.

Standing to the side, I watched her face to see if she would flinch when the surgeon injected the lidocaine around the growth on her chest. Nothing. No reaction. I stepped back and put my head down, not wanting her to see my trembling mouth. I was hoping Melissa would cry, scream, become red-faced, or show some emotions. All reactions any infant or toddler would have. But I knew her passivity was a symptom that children in institutions sometimes develop when little or no attention is paid to them. Why cry if no one will comfort you or address your needs? When it was over, and the Velcro straps had been removed, I picked her up and noticed a small teardrop that had pooled in a little fold of skin under her right eye. Many months later, I noticed a similar little teardrop in the same spot in her passport picture.

The pathology report came back, and the growth was an unusually large wart: "Molluska Contagiosa," a contagious viral wart condition, most likely picked up in the Korean children's orphanage but not anything more serious.

Breadcrumbs

Even though I had a wealth of babysitters at the compound, I was struggling to give Melissa and Jason the diverse attention they needed. Melissa wanted quiet, reassuring snuggles, while Jason would rebuff hugs and kisses, and was constantly in motion.

At the age of three, Jason had been diagnosed at Children's Hospital Boston with Attention Deficit Disorder, ADD (now called Attention Deficit Hyperactivity Disorder, ADHD), as a part of the preschool screening program to determine if he had any learning disorders. The parenting tools Jack and I had used for Matthew hadn't been working for Jason. He was an enigma to us. He had bumped his head pretty hard one day when he was about two-and-a-half years old, and when I tried to scoop him up and comfort him, he struggled and broke loose from my grip, running around the house with teeth gritted crying, "Grrr, grrr, grrr." That became his way to deal with pain—run or jump around, and *for God's sake don't touch me!*

Parenting skills be damned. We were just trying to understand our three-year-old and not constantly beat him down with "Don't touch, don't run, don't move, don't, don't, don't…" I didn't want Jason somehow to internalize that. I believed that if we gave him too many negative reproaches, he would think he was a "bad" boy. I thought if he could see himself in books through the lens of mischievous, yet good characters, it might negate all the "don'ts" of the day. So, *Rotten Ralph*, *No Kiss for Mother*, and *Wind in the Willows* became our misadventure bedtime stories.

At Children's Hospital, they made me wait in an examination room with Jason for quite a while. In that time, he explored the boxes of examining gloves, tongue depressors, tried to get hold of the otoscope and ophthalmoscope, pulled over a chair to look out the window, and crawled on the examining table, wrinkling and tearing the paper covering.

The doctor opened the door, stood in the doorway with his hand still on the door handle, looked around, and smiled at me with a wide, warm grin on his face. "Well, he really tore up the place discovering everything, didn't he?" I felt an immediate release after a long, tense wait. I told the doctor about our observation of how sugar and possibly food coloring affected Jason's activity, and how we managed his behavior. He didn't think medication was necessary.

But two years later, with Melissa's fear of loud noises and roughhousing, it was impossible to expect Jason to play inside quietly. I thought I had the perfect solution:

"Jason, how would you like to take swimming lessons at the 'Y'?"

"Yeah! Really, can I?"

"Yes, but we have to go to the Y to sign you up first."

Once at the Y, I opened the main door and before I could grab his hand, Jason bolted down the hall and disappeared around the corner. Seconds later, he ran back to me and said, "It's not here!"

"Of course it's here, hon, you ran right by it."

He ran down the hall again and returned.

"No, it's not here!"

"Didn't you see the pool through the big windows?"

"Yeah, but where's the piano?"

"The piano?"

"Yes!"

I stooped down to his eye level and held both his hands.

"Jason. Jason, look at me. Do you want to take *piano* lessons?"

He glanced at me quickly, sounded frustrated, and said, "Yes!" Trying to pull away from me, he kept looking around. Where's the piano, Mom?"

I stood up and took his hand. "C'mon let's go."

He began his litany of questions immediately: "Are we going home? Are we going to find the piano? Mom? Mom? Can I see the piano? Can I play it? Where are we going…?"

Holding his sweaty hand, I looked down at his shiny black hair and smiled; we had an old upright piano that he had always liked playing around on, and evidently when he had heard the word "lessons," he had missed the fact that I was talking about *swimming* lessons.

I drove to our town hall and located the community bulletin board inside the main door. I found a notice advertising piano lessons for children and adults and tore off a tab at the bottom with the teacher's name and telephone number. I called as soon as we got home.

"What grade is he in?" she asked.

"He's in kindergarten."

"I don't take students until they're old enough to read."

Jason was looking up at me, and I could see the intensity in his eyes. He was standing still, watching me closely, trying to hear the conversation.

"Can I bring him to you and let you decide if he's too young?"

I watched from the sofa as the teacher placed Jason's little fingers on the keys. Pointing to the notes in a children's music book, she said, "See that note there? That's this key here. It's called C." And so on through D, E, F, G, A, B. She asked him to play what he saw on the page. He sat practically motionless on the piano bench and played the entire little song. He couldn't read the words to the song, but he could read the notes. The teacher turned to me and said, "I'll take him."

Who is this child? Is this something that makes him tick?

But what made Melissa tick? Child psychology courses from nursing school were still fresh in my mind, and I found myself absorbed by the mystery of Melissa's past and how it was affecting her development. Each day gave me a clue to her past, a developmental gain to celebrate, or a new issue to overcome. We were trying to understand where she was emotionally and developmentally.

I jotted down any incident or observation that seemed pertinent. For instance, one day I brought her to our church rectory to meet with the priest who was helping us plan her baptism. I carried Melissa into the church office and put her down. The priest rose from his desk and came forward to greet us. But instead of a warm greeting, he halted and stood in place, his smile morphing from alarm to embarrassment. I turned around just in time to see Melissa backing away from him in abject terror. I had never seen this look of fear on her, at least not to this degree. I picked her up and held her tightly. A man wearing a black cassock—was his appearance triggering a bad memory? Was this part of the "fear of men" that Jean had warned us about? The priest felt terrible; however, to my surprise, Melissa quickly calmed down.

Another incident occurred after Jack had returned from a five-day business trip. I was talking to Jack as he was shaving in the bathroom, and Melissa was hugging his leg. Trying to gain a little more space, Jack said, "Missy, let Daddy shave. Go see Mommy." He unclasped her hands around his leg and nudged her into the hallway where I was standing. Jack glanced back in the mirror and didn't see what happened next. Melissa turned and stared at Jack as if in disbelief. She put her fingers to her mouth, pushed her lower lip out like she was going to cry, and stopped breathing. Her lips turned blue, her eyes rolled back, and she fell backward. I grabbed her just before she hit the floor.

Socially, Melissa wanted to be around kids, but, unless someone did something with her, she just stood by and watched. Matthew had picked up on this and discovered she loved playing a silly game he called "mashed potatoes." "C'mon, Melissa, climb up here. You can do it." He would lie down on the sofa and would help Melissa climb up on his chest. "Hold on, we're gonna get mashed!" he'd say, and the two would "fall off" and roll on the rug. Depending on who landed on top, Matthew would cry out, "Who's the mashed potatoes?" Melissa couldn't talk yet but would laugh with delight every time he did this.

She also loved water. When I put Melissa and Jason in for a bath at night, if she got her face wet, or even if her head went under the water, instead of panic and tears or fearful looks, she would erupt in giggles—no fear!

Before Melissa's adoption was final, our social worker stopped by for her last home visit. As she gathered up her purse and papers to leave, she said, "I thought Melissa would be talking by now. It could be that her physical and emotional trauma might have been so great that she's not speaking as a defense mechanism." I agreed with her. However, I was not yet concerned about the problem, thinking it was just a matter of time and love. Melissa understood what was being said and was responding appropriately, but for whatever reason, she could not or would not talk.

One night, when I was lying down in our bedroom waiting for Melissa to fall asleep, I heard something that made me sit up. I thought I heard her say a very soft "beh-beh." I watched in semi-darkness as she repeated, "beh-beh." So, she *could* make sounds. I tiptoed over to the crib and whispered "beh-beh" to her, but she just looked back at me. She didn't make another sound until two weeks later, when I heard her say something that sounded like "meh" in her crib. It seemed she liked the safety and quiet of her crib to try out these new sounds, because she would shake her head "no" if anyone tried to get her to talk. She was making the "heh" sound for "hi" and "hot," "beh" sound for "baby" and "drink," and "meh" for "mama." But there were no vowel sounds. It appeared at times like she genuinely didn't know how to form the sounds or words, and other times like she was refusing to make any sounds.

In addition to her fear of abandonment and physical harm, food was another big issue. Audrey had written that Melissa overate the first day she was with them and had vomited after the meal. With us, Melissa acted as if every meal would be her last. Sitting in her highchair, she would pull her dish close to her and slowly eat everything on it—guaranteeing the last remnants would be stone cold. If any food fell to the floor, she would lean over the side of the highchair and point to the scrap until it was picked up and returned to her plate. She would also cry or hold her breath if we took her plate away before she had finished.

I was cleaning the kitchen one day when I saw Melissa pulling on the dishwasher handle. I stopped and watched because I'd never seen her do anything with such determination before. She was trying to open the dishwasher, and she did. The door fell open, scaring her momentarily, but then she picked out a dirty dish and started licking it. Jason saw her and made a production out of the "grossness" of it, but I shooed him away and took the dish from her.

Melissa's documentation said she had suffered from anorexia and malnutrition while in Korea. Infant anorexia is usually caused by deprivation of attention and care, and it had progressed to failure to thrive in Melissa's case. Now that she was surrounded by continual attention and love, she was catching up with growth spurts and was slowly learning new skills. However, it seemed like she was still trying to fill an empty spot in her psyche with food. Maybe she was using food to soothe her emotional traumas, but I suspected it was due to past hunger. I think James Baldwin captured this pathos perfectly when he wrote about himself in *Notes of a Native Son,* "I love to eat and drink—it's my melancholy conviction that I've scarcely ever had enough to eat, (this is because it's *impossible* to eat enough if you're worried about the next meal)..." So, on a very non-scientific level—a mother's level—I thought Melissa still didn't feel safe enough to assume she would get fed again or fed enough. She was leaving little breadcrumbs for us to discover. If only we could understand her past and what she could and couldn't do—then maybe, we could fix it. Yes, maybe we could fix it.

No Dead-End Streets

I was ready. Juggling Melissa on my hip, I threw my pocketbook and an overstuffed bag of diapers, juice containers, snacks, and an extra set of clothes on the front seat of the car. Jack was working, so I was the one who had to drive to Boston for Melissa's medical appointments at Massachusetts General Hospital, MGH, and Shriners Hospital.

Putting Melissa down, I made sure her jacket and clothes were smooth and not crumpled around her. That was important. Seeing no loose tags or strings, I buckled her into the car seat. The first time I took her on a small errand in the car, she started fussing. I could hear her making some sounds, and in the rearview mirror, I could see that something was wrong. Her face was red, there were sweat beads on her face, and she was tugging on the sleeve of her jacket. I pulled into a small shopping center parking lot, got out of the car, and opened the back door. What was the problem? Her arm and wrist looked all right, and then I saw it: It was a piece of thread hanging from the cuff of her jacket. That was the problem. I was finding out it was one of her little quirks. Loose strings, threads, hanging pieces of tape, paper, anything that seemed to have a free end, Melissa felt compelled to pull it off and would get upset if she couldn't. I couldn't afford a repeat on this trip.

Around 300 years ago, houses in Boston were erected willy-nilly, and streets emerged wherever houses or businesses sprang up, so it's easy to understand how the urban myth developed that the streets of Boston were built upon a maze of cow paths. Anyone who has ever driven into Boston will tell you there's no making sense of a lot of street signs in the old Beacon Hill section of town, and to make it even more confusing, throw in one-way streets. It's no exaggeration that you could drive around and around on narrow one-way streets until you give up, admitting "you just can't get there from here!" One wrong turn and your trip could take you twenty to thirty minutes longer. This trip needed to go smoothly. I did not want to end up on a narrow, one-way street with a fussy, exasperated toddler who couldn't tell me what was bothering her, while I had no place to pull over.

Boston Driver Lesson #1: When merging into another lane, put your lane indicator light on, and at the first small opening of space between cars in traffic, MOVE! There is no polite, "wait your turn." Boston drivers are a dogged breed, and it's best to follow suit, so, exiting off route 93 S into Boston, I got the car into the far-right lane to get onto Storrow Drive, and quickly merged into the left lane, which led onto a small overpass, taking a sharp left turn at the bottom of the overpass into the parking lot of MGH. Trying to keep my adrenaline in check, I changed Melissa's diaper in the car, then we made our way through the parking lot and into the hospital.

Melissa was now three feet tall, twenty-nine pounds, and wearing a size-three toddler outfit. Her pixie hairstyle had grown out; she had bangs, and her hair was just long enough to put into two small black pigtails, which were held together by red-and-white Hello Kitty hair elastics. Navigating another maze and letting her walk by herself in her wide, "just-learning-to-walk" gait, we eventually found the Pediatric Neurology Department.

We needed to have Melissa tested to determine what her school needs would be and what programs would be beneficial for her. We expected that she would "catch up" developmentally and didn't want to waste any time making that happen. The doctor ordered a battery of tests for the upcoming weeks: CT scan, EEG, speech and language evaluation, and psychometric testing—a measurement of intelligence and behavior.

Shriners Hospital for Children in Boston specializes in free burn care for children from all over the world. After we entered it via an underground tunnel connecting the two hospitals, a Shriner volunteer wearing the well-known red fez greeted Melissa immediately. He made a big deal of Melissa; to be fair, the volunteers did this for every little patient. He escorted her to the burn clinic waiting room where, unlike the neurologist's office, there were no toys. It was a large open area with an extended L-shaped sofa seating arrangement. There were about twelve patients in the waiting room.

The wait was long, which gave me ample time to observe the children. This clinic was not for the faint of heart. In the waiting room, there were children who were disfigured; some mildly, some horribly, but all no longer resembling that "perfect" child they had once been. Beautiful soft skin turned to leathery, wrinkled scar tissue. Limbs bandaged in ways that belied missing hands, fingers, or toes. Pressure "masks" on tiny faces, pressure gloves on little hands, arm dressings, leg dressings, scalp dressings, scalp tissue expanders—grotesque, temporary, balloon-like "growths" on small heads. It was almost too hard to bear, yet here were these children, some as young as infants, others up to high school age, all calm, with no one recoiling at their appearances. I watched Melissa as she wandered around near me. I don't know if anything frightened her because she didn't seem to react to any of it, for which I was thankful. However, to me it was frankly jarring and sad.

We finally saw the surgeon. Melissa would need a graft on her right thigh, surgery to loosen the scar tissue behind her knees, and reconstructive surgery on her lower right leg. They decided she was still too emotionally fragile to have any surgery. I put Melissa's diaper and clothes back on and set her down. On our way out of the examining area, a nurse ran after me. "Mrs. Tumminello!" I turned around. "Our weekly support group is about to begin. Can you stay? I really think you should."

Shriners provided childcare for the attending parents, and Melissa had already wandered into the room full of other children—she was drawn to the kids, not the toys. Seeing her happy for the moment, I reluctantly agreed, but felt I had no immediate need and indeed felt humbled and thankful that our family had been spared the horrible trauma of experiencing a burn injury to a child and the painful recovery—if there had been one. In the meeting room, there was the usual circle of chairs and an assortment of parents and/or guardians. The group consisted almost entirely of women, and I don't think anything dramatic was discussed because I recall little of the meeting. My mind was elsewhere. I was thinking of that CT scan that the neurologist had ordered across the street at MGH.

What would it reveal? Somehow, I just felt the more appropriate support group would not be with burn patient families, but with parents of children with disabilities.

The CT scan of Melissa's brain found some minor abnormalities of unknown etiology. I poured over the report countless times. The nurse in me was obsessed with trying to figure out the anomaly on the scan. Was that deficit causing all these problems? Did something else happen to her as an infant? Did she also experience any physical trauma to her head? After a few months of reading about brain injuries and asking doctors, I decided I needed to let this go. Nobody could tell us. Melissa had experienced great physical and emotional trauma. As a mother, I saw the daily, sometimes hourly, looks of fear on her face. I could comfort her and reassure her, but I could never erase the harm done to her.

What mattered now was what we were going to do about it. Would she be able to catch up? What would Melissa's future look like? Would anybody be able to tell us that? We were still holding on to the hope that love and caring would take care of the failure-to-thrive issues and the motor and cognitive deficits Melissa was exhibiting, but that hope was fading.

Are You Listening?

With all the challenges of Melissa's adoption, I sought respite in the rare quiet moments of the day or evening, in my yard. It had the power to either quiet most of my fears or worries, or to validate my joy: The bright yellow leaves of the giant ash trees in the fall, the worn stone walls, the birch trees, the hemlocks silhouetted in winter moonlight, the chickadee chattering, the *ssshhhh* of wind rustling through tree leaves in summer, and even the blue jays cawing on frigid winter days, all of it—no matter the season—brought beauty, calm, and happiness. This small piece of land had such a hold on me. My sister shared the same affection for it. You could find her on many summer and fall afternoons, sitting on an old wooden bench under a clump of deciduous trees near the hemlocks, looking out over the field to her garden and bird feeders.

One sultry summer night, with all the windows open, I was awakened by a noise I couldn't immediately make out. I got up and went to the bedroom window. *Is it a bird?* It was well past midnight, but also well before sunrise. Everyone was asleep, so I slipped out to the front porch and down the stone steps toward the ceaseless birdsong. It seemed to be coming from the hemlock trees. There was a full moon, so I walked in the moonlit field between our house and my parents' house. I came around the stand of trees and saw my sister walking up from her house, approaching from the other side of the trees. There we were. The two of us in our nightgowns; the only ones who had heard the frenetic trill of the mockingbird's beautiful song. The trees, the moonlight, the mockingbird, the serenade…all just wondrous.

Sometimes, while daydreaming, I tried to imagine what the land had been like one hundred or more years earlier. Who had tilled the land? Who had dug the stone well? Who had planted the apple trees—the Baldwins, Macintosh, and Gravensteins? And when? What was their story? And what was the story of my childhood favorite, the pear-apple tree? I didn't exactly know what kind of tree it was—nobody did. I called it the pear-apple tree because the large yellow-and-pink-tinged fruit had a juicy pear flavor. There had been no other trees like it. Just this beloved, solitary apple tree. As a child, I had thought of it as belonging only to me. My tree. Mine.

Even though she couldn't speak, Melissa made an announcement that summer. Before it happened, I had been driving her back and forth to speech and occupational therapy at one of our local hospitals, and I was nearly home one day when she started to cry. Glancing back at her, I could see her face was dark pink and covered with sweat. It was a hot day, and in those days, cars didn't have air-conditioning vents in the back seats. This time, I knew what the problem was. Heat affected Melissa. She had no sweat glands on the parts of her body that were burned, which made her more susceptible to heat exhaustion. As soon as I parked the car in the driveway, I pulled Melissa out of her car seat and ran into the bathroom to cool her down.

For the rest of the summer, if it was a hot day, as soon as we arrived home, I would plunk her down in a little blue plastic kiddie pool we had placed next to the driveway. I was mildly stressed at these moments, but I didn't want Melissa to see it in my face. I didn't want her to associate water, which she loved, with anything terrible, so we made a game of it. I'm guessing it worked, because one day when the boys and I were out by the pool and I was trying to get the wet leaves out of the skimmer net, I heard Matthew yell, "Mom!" I looked over. Melissa was in the water and sinking. I wasn't close enough to grab her, so I ran and leapt into the pool with sneakers, jeans, and a sweatshirt on. Before I could get to her, she came to the surface, looked at me wide-eyed with disbelief, and silently slipped under the water again. I grabbed her and handed her up to Matthew. "Mom, she just walked over to the edge and stepped off!" he cried. Jason thought my performance was hysterical. Matthew and I were shaken but not surprised—and Melissa? She wasn't upset at all. I think she was announcing, *Forget about learning to talk; I just want to learn to swim.*

It was during one particular occupational therapy session that it hit me. I watched as the therapist stood behind Melissa, straddling her feet, and guiding her arms in an underhanded ball-throwing style. "Throw the ball, Melissa, let go of it." Over and over, she tried to get her to throw the ball. That evening, with Jason and Melissa asleep, and Matthew doing homework in his room, I poured my usual cup of tea and sat down on the couch with Jack. "You know, I watched Melissa try to throw a ball today. She knew what she wanted to do but couldn't get her body to cooperate—it was like she was a stroke patient."

"A stroke patient? What do you mean?"

"Well, with a lot of therapy, some patients recover their motor skills. Why can't Melissa? Maybe we could 'rewire' her brain to recover them." Jack listened to my hypothesis.

"Hmm," he said. "I guess that makes sense. So, what do we do?"

"We get to work."

Even if the stroke comparison was all wrong, it was enough to give me hope. I needed to believe in Melissa. *We* needed to believe in Melissa. Puzzles, blocks, tricycles—everything she did now had a purpose. She was four years old, and ordinary childhood learning could not be taken for granted. My mother and sister jumped on board to help. If Melissa was at my mother's when they were cooking (which was a lot—my mom and sister cooked from scratch every day), they would pull a kitchen chair over to the counter and make sure Melissa could mix, stir, or add ingredients.

A friend of ours once told me that seeing all the smudgy little fingerprints of her children on the window above their living room couch made her happy. This was where her children waved goodbye to Daddy every morning. So, all those gouges on the legs of our sofa from Melissa's tricycle gave me the same feeling. It made me happy—*she's learning.*

It took all summer, but Melissa's speech therapist finally taught her how to make vowel sounds. Now she would be able to learn words. We were thrilled. Not so thrilling was the additional medical documentation from the summer's therapy sessions that showed that Melissa has speech and motor apraxia coupled with a sensory disorder that complicated the motor apraxia. She has visual-motor integration difficulties as well.

Speech apraxia is a neurological condition that can affect one's ability to form words—Melissa knew what she wanted to say but getting the muscles in her throat and around her mouth to work was very difficult. Motor apraxia similarly affects the muscles in one's arms and legs, which in Melissa's case was compounded by the proprioception problem. Proprioception is the ability to sense one's body's location, motion, and actions without thinking consciously about it. We don't think about our feet if we're running or walking and want to jump over a puddle. We just know they're on the ground. Melissa had to *think* about where her feet were. I witnessed a simple example of this problem when Melissa's occupational therapist asked her, "Where are your feet, Melissa?" Melissa was sitting at a small table where she could not see her legs or feet. Her eyes scanned the tabletop over and over, looking for her feet. She didn't know. Visual-motor integration—the ability to coordinate what one sees into gross- or fine-motor skills, such as printing a letter, tying a shoe, drawing a picture, or buttoning a shirt would become more problematic as she grew older.

It was an ugly list. All her deficits, we thought, were now uncovered. Melissa was at the bottom of a hole and the only way out was to help her grab on to that skill-ladder and tackle each rung. We knew any gains would be slow and would not happen on their own. Pretty much everything Melissa attempted to do would be a struggle, requiring deliberate thought on her part, and work and patience on ours. We not only needed the patience to wait for her to learn skills, but also the patience to take the time to see what she was trying to tell us about herself.

Jason was revealing something about himself too. Playing the piano had a calming effect on him, and it wasn't unusual for him to break away from an activity multiple times during the day and run to the piano. He'd sit quietly on the piano bench, and with his head moving sideways back and forth, he'd play his little ditties. They weren't his piano assignments. They were just little tunes he made up as he went along. He was in his "zone." It seemed like he instinctively knew when he was getting overstimulated, and playing the piano quieted him down.

But one afternoon, I was having an extremely difficult time managing him. He was a whirlwind of energy, running around the house, jumping from chairs and sofas, scattering Legos and Matchbox cars. It seemed all I could do was run after him, trying to make sure he didn't hurt himself or Melissa, or destroy whatever toy or object he picked up. There was fury in his eyes. The day's climax came when he ran over to the piano and started banging on the keys. Bang, bang, bang. Run, run, run. Bang, bang, bang. Something was wrong. I called my mother.

"Mom, did Jason have anything to eat or drink when he came down there this morning?"

"I don't think so. Why? What's the matter? Is he sick?"

"No, but I can't get him to stop running around. He's tearing up the place."

"Hold on," she said. I heard her open the refrigerator door and then shout, "Erin, come here." There was a popular kids' blue-colored fruit drink container in the fridge, and she told me Erin had given some to Jason. I hung up. A sugar-laced, artificial drink was exploding in Jason's brain. He was out of control.

Bang, bang, bang.

I grabbed him by the shoulders, bent down, and shook him. "Jason! Look at me. You don't feel good right now, right? Do you?"

"Grrr, let me go!"

"Jason, Jason, listen. You had some of Erin's tropical punch, didn't you? That's what is making you feel this way!"

There was perspiration running down his face, and his darting eyes suddenly focused on me. "It's okay, honey. You don't want to feel this way again, do you?"

At that moment, I wanted him to understand the connection between the fruit drink and his profound irritability. I just knew he had to understand his behavior and how ADD affected his actions, and that fruit drink offered a dramatic example that a six-year-old might be able to grasp. I was afraid his ADD was going to be a lifelong struggle, and maybe just as challenging as Melissa's problems.

At dinner, Jason was quiet and rubbing his right eye with the back of his hand, a sure sign that sleep was not too far off. Jack said, "He's really quiet tonight, isn't he?"

I looked at Jack and then Matthew, and then back to Jack.

"Quiet? He's exhausted!"

Before Jason had arrived, we had been smug about our parenting skills. After all, we had raised the perfect child—Matthew. Easy-going and quiet, he never seemed to break the rules. Just one reminder not to touch or do something was all he needed. When he was almost five years old, I had given him a dime one day, to buy a popsicle when he heard the familiar kiddie-tune jingle of the ice-cream truck. He flew out the door, and I went to the bedroom window to watch. We lived in a subdivision, so the street was pretty quiet, and there he stood, dime in hand, at the edge of our yard, with the ice-cream truck parked across the street. He didn't know what to do. I had to call out to him that it was okay to cross the street. He knew he wasn't supposed to cross the street alone—that was the rule.

Rules didn't carry much meaning for Erin, though. She thought it was just fine to cut the legs off her Dapper Dan doll, scribble on her other dolls with Magic Markers, and write on chalkboards with crayon, making my mother almost apoplectic. As a result, Erin was the dominant one when she and Matthew played together. One day, my mother and I were watching them play outside. They were told to take turns riding her tricycle. Erin quickly showed us her version of taking turns: "Matthew, I'll ride down, and you can ride up the driveway." At that age, they were a Charlie-Brown-and-Lucy duo—Matthew forever trying to do the right thing, and Erin, his tormentor. Looking back, Erin would have been the dominant one no matter what—a take-charge person, just like my mom. Years later, it would be her take-charge spunk and moxie that would get our family through a terribly dark time.

How Can I Make It Better?

Melissa and her pre-kindergarten classmates went to the YMCA pool once a week for physical therapy. The goal for Melissa was to help with "bilateral gross motor skills"—to get her to use both sides of her body—arms and legs. The goal for Jack and me was for her to learn how to swim.

The parents, mostly mothers, were invited to the last day for award ceremonies. I brought my camera, not sure what I would see. We had been asking Melissa if she could swim, and she always replied, "Yes," (she had about a twenty-five-word vocabulary now) but we were never sure if she really could. The resource teacher greeted the parents in the steamy pool area and instructed us to stand along one side of the pool. The high school volunteers were in the shallow end of the pool, and the children were lined up on the other side of the pool, some holding kickboards and looking a little frightened. Melissa had on her favorite floral-covered bathing suit with a ruffle along the top edge. She spotted me and beamed a huge smile. Her turn came. She walked to the pool edge, jumped into the water, gave a little hop with her foot, stretched her arms out in front of her, and swam to the waiting volunteer at the other side of the pool. Twenty-five yards she swam, all by herself, and giggling. And I didn't get one picture of it.

I was riveted. I didn't want to take my eyes off her for even a moment. At last, something she could excel in that didn't produce tears—at least not for her.

But perhaps the one thing that delighted Melissa the most that year was her ability to do a somersault. Dressed in a little pink tutu, pink tights, and pink ballet slippers, she got to do a somersault as part of the adaptive physical education end-of-year "Circus Show" for the parents.

A few days after that school production, we had an interesting "discussion" with Melissa: It was a hot, muggy day, and Jack and I were sitting on a grassy incline in our backyard enjoying the shade and hoping a faint breeze would pick up. Melissa, barefoot and dressed in a little, pale-green summer dress, was showing us her somersaults. I saw how tight and shiny the skin behind her knees was and could tell by her wince that the adhesions hurt her. On an impulse, I pointed to her burns and asked: "What happened?" We had never talked to her about them, but I thought she might have enough vocabulary now to tell us something. We had never speculated aloud in front of Melissa about what might have caused her burns—if Child Psychology classes had taught me anything, it was that asking a child a leading or highly suggestive question could produce a memory of something that had never happened. (This fact was confirmed when I watched the TV news frenzy of the McMartin Preschool Sexual Abuse Scandal that began just a few months later, in August, 1983.) So, holding my breath a little, and giving Melissa all the time she needed, I waited for her answer. Her smile disappeared, and she said only two words: "wet fire."

"Wet fire." Jack and I looked at each other. It made sense. Melissa's burns were on the exposed parts of her legs, feet, and buttocks that would be burned if a hot liquid spilled, or worse, was poured on her. The other, more troubling thought I had was— Melissa remembers something. Had that been her nightmare months earlier when she was inconsolable, and we had to take her into our bed for the night? We decided we would not delve into this any further. It would do no good. It would be speculation on our part and revisiting trauma for Melissa. But sometimes I'd pick her up and look into her eyes and wonder: *What do you know? What do you remember, baby? How can I make it better for you?* She was like a fragile seedling pushing up through the heavy soil of trauma, looking for sunlight.

Over the next few years, Melissa's fear of sudden loud noises (her teacher had to pick her up and carry her out during the first fire alarm drill) and normal childhood rowdiness was abating. She mingled easily with other children and enjoyed showing everyone at home her school papers adorned with stickers and stars. But most importantly, she had started talking and putting words into sentences. Except for math skills—which were almost nonexistent—Melissa continued to make slow but steady progress in all her academic and physical goals. At home, the thinking was that she would do as many daily activities as she could: taking a shower, getting dressed, brushing her teeth, setting the table, making her bed, and following multistep directions, etc. But it was not without pushback.

"C'mon, Melissa, let's go. We need to get to the hairdressers!"

"Why?"

"So you can get your hair cut."

"I don't want to."

"Don't you want to brush and wash your hair all by yourself?"

"I don't want to cut my hair!"

"I know you don't, but you're going to have a pretty haircut, and it's going to be easy to take care of. Now c'mon, get in the car."

Shortly after this trip to the hairdresser's, Melissa got out of the shower one evening with only the right side of her head shampooed. The other side was practically dry (she was still favoring the right side of her body, and getting both hands to work simultaneously continued to be a problem). I put my hands on the top of her shoulders and guided her back to the bathroom mirror. "Look," I said. She laughed when she saw herself. "This is why you got your hair cut."

By age ten, I felt Melissa had enough verbal and comprehension skills to make her First Communion, so I went to our church to register her for Confraternity of Christian Doctrine (CCD) classes and spoke to the administrator to explain Melissa's learning style: If Melissa was trying to tell you a story, she could lose her train of thought easily, and sometimes get stuck either trying to think of a word, or working out how to say a word and would keep repeating the last two or three words over and over, until she either remembered it or thought of another word or a way to tell us what she wanted to say. Her repetitions resembled stuttering, in that she knew what she wanted to say, but it just wasn't coming out. For instance: She might say, "Nana and I made," then close her eyes in concentration, and say, "Nana and I made, Nana and I made, we made chocolate chip cookies."

The CCD administrator listened to me and then said, "I'm sorry; we can't accommodate her."

"Why?" I replied. "She understands everything you are saying to her. If you ask her a question, and if it's a simple answer, she'll be able to answer it. She won't be able to write answers, but she can if it's take-home, and she has extra time."

"No, I'm sorry. We're not set up for that."

"I can sit in the back of the room and help her if the instructor agrees."

"No, I'm afraid we can't do that."

I left. There are some fights you have to walk away from. You can't win the "hearts and attitudes" if you're only given one chance, and this woman had decided.

I drove to St. Irene's, a small, chapel-like church in a nearby rural town, and talked to the religious instructor. She was happy to accommodate Melissa—no reservations or hesitations. Her teacher made her feel like she belonged in that class. Melissa understood the stories, was able to answer simple questions, and a group of seven- and eight-year-olds were exposed to someone who looked and spoke a little differently than they.

That fall, we had attended mass at St. Irene's again, and at the end of the ceremony, the pastor, Father Byrne, announced he was looking for new altar boys. Walking out of the church, Jason suddenly stopped and declared, "I want to be an altar boy."

"What! Jason, this isn't even our parish," Jack said.

"But I want to be an altar boy!"

Jack and I looked at each other. Oh boy, here it comes. This is Jason, we thought. The devilish child! Who were we to object if he wanted to do this?

"Well, if you want to be an altar boy, you'll have to talk to Father Byrne," Jack said.

"Okay."

From our limited observation of him, Father Byrne was a tall, thin, elderly, seemingly crotchety, impatient priest. We were sure he would not be receptive to Jason's request. Jack, Matthew, Melissa, and I stayed behind in the pew and watched the exchange. Father Byrne stood in the middle of the aisle, looked down at ten-year-old Jason, and gave him a lecture.

"If you want to be an altar boy, you need to show up for practice and serve at your scheduled masses. I don't want you to waste my time if you're not serious."

"Okay!" said Jason with a gleam in his eyes.

With a faint smile on his face, Father Byrne glanced over at Jack and me. Maybe he wasn't so crotchety after all, I thought. Father Byrne didn't intimidate Jason. The other altar boys were quiet and treated the priest respectfully—not Jason. It was at a memorable Christmas mass a few months later that Jason exhibited that fact. The church was tiny, and the altar was only steps away from the front pews. The mass was about to begin, and Father Byrne was standing behind Jason and another young altar boy in the sacristy doorway. The organist started a hymn, and Father Byrne nudged Jason to begin the eight-step procession to the altar. Jason held up his wrist, which displayed his new Christmas present—a digital watch, and in his not-so-quiet whisper-voice said, "No, we've got two more minutes." After about a second of shock, the entire congregation burst out laughing, including Father Byrne, who laughed, patted Jason's head, and said, "No, Jason, go."

Father Byrne seemed to love the same impishness that Dad did. He gave away his feelings one time when during his sermon about heeding the call to serve God, Father looked over at the two altar boys and said, "Right, Jason?" Jason had been fiddling with the cross around his neck and had wound it around the cord until the cord was a tight and twisted mess. The congregants chuckled, and I groaned (I had been watching and trying to get Jason's eye so I could mouth "stop it!" to him). I had never heard a priest interject a remark to an altar boy in the middle of a sermon. It sounds corny, but to me, in the intimacy of that small church, I felt like we were all at the dinner table, and Father was trying to guide his children with a dinner discussion and fatherly reprobation.

We had always liked the feeling of this church. There was an intimacy about it. One Sunday, Father Byrne announced the name of a newly baptized child. The child's family was seated a few rows in front of us, and the father, who was holding his sleeping newborn, did something I had never seen before in a Catholic Church; he raised the infant up high for all to see. It was as if he was offering her up to God and the congregation to welcome and embrace her with love. I have never forgotten that beautiful moment. Such a different experience from our former, large, impersonal church. St. Irene's became our new parish. We felt welcomed into this community. Many, many times, Father Byrne said from the pulpit, "I never want to drive anyone away from the church by either my actions or words." He was a good man with a kind heart. He had a simple philosophy: We are all family. Love each other. Accept and include everyone. So, that spring, it was both fitting and comforting that St. Irene's welcomed Melissa as a new communicant and said goodbye to Dad.

Dad had died that spring in 1986. He had congestive heart disease and grew weaker and weaker until his heart could no longer support him. "No more hospitals," he told me one day. I was standing in front of him in the dining room. "I promise, Dad, no more hospitals." Mom had converted the sunny dining room into a bedroom. There were large windows on three sides. From his recliner, Dad could see the front yard, and looking out the French door next to his armchair, he could see the backyard, where an orange-flowered trumpet vine was threatening to overtake the nearby gate he had built years earlier. And finally, to Dad's right, he could see the side field—which our driveway now bisected.

"What more could I ask for?" he said to me. "I can sit here, look out, and see the kids every day."

"Dad, do you realize you and Mom got to watch all your grandchildren grow up in this house? That's a gift, you know."

He smiled weakly at that thought and closed his eyes. I looked down at him. He looked so small. A blanket covered his legs, a plaid flannel shirt covered his shrunken frame, and a mop of gray had replaced his thick black hair. His spirit was ebbing away from me. But he was at peace—surrounded by everything he loved. I stood in the silence and gazed above his head to the field beyond—his yard, our yard. A misty memory emerged: I was twelve years old and standing with Dad in the field. Luther, our next-door neighbor, was walking toward us. He was wearing a crumpled tan field hat, smoking his pipe, and had his ever-present German Shepherd by his side. Luther was a weathered old fellow who came from a long line of New England stock with deep roots in our town. He hunted, fished, had a vegetable garden, fruit trees, a grapevine, and a beehive. He was telling Dad about our land and the fading apple orchard. The three of us were walking through the field up to the apple trees. He was going to show something to Dad…but my reverie quickly dissipated—the hiss from Dad's oxygen machine returning me to the present. Luther was long dead, but his presence was still strongly felt.

I left Dad to his dreams.

A few nights later, for some unremembered reason, my mother and sister invited us over for dinner. My sister Pat, her husband, "Buzz," Jack, Matthew, Jason, Melissa, and I were all there. We lingered after dinner, and before we left, said goodnight to Dad, who was in bed.

Mom called a few hours later and gave us the news.

High Anxiety

Dad and Father Byrne might have thought Jason's antics were amusing, but for me, dealing with his hyperactivity day in and day out was a challenge. His escapades were relentless. When he was younger, most of them had been humorous. One morning when he was about five years old, I had to get him ready for school, but he wasn't in his bed. We searched the whole house, called to see if he had gone to my mother's house, and were about to scour the neighborhood when I decided to check his room again. No sight of him, but then I spotted it; there was a small crib in his bedroom that I had reused for all the stuffed animals, and there, under the pile of soft toys, was a small hand poking out between the bars of the crib railing. Jason had decided to hide on us. He had gotten the idea from the scene in the movie *ET* when ET hides in the closet among all the toys—the only problem was that he had fallen back to sleep before we could find him.

But Jason's impulsive behavior had been dangerous, too. On vacation at a resort in New Hampshire, Matthew, Jason, Jack, and I, along with some friends, had taken a guided hike through the woods to an outcropping overlooking a notch in the mountains where you could look down and see the road running through the pass, as well as a lovely view of the resort and lake. The resort described the hike as "easy and family friendly." Our college-aged guide had kept urging us on by saying, "It's not far," which had become less and less believable and started to be a joke among us as we trudged upward. Jason, who was five years old, had been continuously running ahead a few yards, and then running back to the group. The entire hike had been in the woods, so we had no idea how close we were to the lookout spot. The guide was just ahead of us, and Jason was a few steps in front of him, when we finally saw the opening in the woods—and the rock ledge ahead. Jack yelled to the guide to grab Jason's hand. He did, but the guide must have thought once Jason saw the edge, he would quiet down, so he let go of his hand. Afraid of heights, Jack dropped to his knees, and began approaching Jason slowly. Everyone in the group froze and watched as Jason scrambled around the rocks to peer over the edge. Jack continued to creep forward until he was close enough to pull him back and put an iron grip on his wrist.

If anyone tried to get Jason to come to them when he was having fun, his first reaction would be to run the other way. On that same vacation, I had been trying to get him out of the pool (he loved to swim and had just learned to dive off the diving board), but when he stepped off the ladder and saw me with a towel, he made a mad dash for the diving board—the high diving board. "Jason, come back here," I yelled. There was no lifeguard, and everyone at the pool was now watching him scramble up the tall ladder. He stepped onto the diving board and looked down at me. I was standing by the ladder at the deep end of the pool and was furious with him. I lowered my voice and said, "Jason, get down from there, it's too high, do you hear me? It's too high, get down." He had that look that told me he was determined. Don't dive—my thought had barely registered when he ran down the board and jumped. Halfway down, he looked at me with wide eyes—he realized he was still falling. He swam to the ladder, and I grabbed his arm and pulled him up. It had scared him. I knew he'd never do it again, at least not on that diving board, and not on that vacation. I'm sure some of the women watching from lounge chairs had been thinking, what a terrible kid, and that mother needs to control her son. Sigh, we would discipline him, lecture him, and monitor him until the next "fun" idea caught his fancy.

We sent Jason to public school for grade six through eight, because the Catholic school he had been attending only went up to grade five. When he discovered all the afterschool activities available to him in the public school, he was thrilled, but he had some reservations. I had to laugh when he had said, "Do you think I'll have many friends in this school?"

"Well, let's see, Jason, you want to join the chess club, math club, and band. What do you think?"

I knew it wouldn't be a problem; he didn't worry about what others thought of him and made friends easily. Jason found it almost incredulous that the school provided music instruction on a variety of instruments. He chose the alto saxophone, so piano lessons were immediately replaced by afterschool music classes. When I dropped him off for his first music class, as he walked away carrying the saxophone case, I heard him say to no one in particular, "I can't believe they gave this to me."

The music director told him that since he had never played

the saxophone, he would have to take lessons for a year before he could join the jazz band. Reluctantly, he agreed. A few weeks later, he came home from school and said, "Mom, the music teacher said I could join the band."

"Really? But I thought…"

"We were practicing an easy song, and when my turn came, I hit a wrong note and it sounded like 'America the Beautiful' to me, so I played that instead."

Getting Jason to sit still had always been next to impossible. It was why he had wanted to be an altar boy; so he could move around and ring the bells. It was also why he had been the catcher on his Little League team; it had kept him busy—he had to think, strategize, and above all, stop talking and pay attention. At parent-teacher meetings, Jack and I were invariably met with the same message: his teachers would begin by saying that he was smart and gets good grades, and then add, "but he talks too much and doesn't pay attention." At one meeting, his sixth-grade teacher was telling us about his inattention and talking in the back of the classroom. She wasn't telling us anything we didn't already know, but then she said, "The thing is, every time I stop and ask him what I just said, he's always able to answer me." We understood her frustration, but knew that sitting in the same seat, in the same classroom, with the same teacher, all day was problematic.

Our kitchen wall bore the evidence of his constant movement. We had bought an extra-long cord for the kitchen phone, which hung adjacent to a corner wall. When Jason was on the phone, he would pace back and forth and around the corner, leaving markings all along the corner's edge where the cord had rubbed against the paint. I had asked him one day why he did that, and he had said, "Because I can concentrate better." It might seem strange to some, but those markings on the corner of the wall, just like the markings on the sofa legs from Melissa's tricycle, kindled the same feelings in me—my intense love for him.

The Sign of Change

Kelly's mother and I were sitting in our usual seats in front of the large, fogged-up convex bubble window watching the girls during their swimming lessons. Kelly was a vivacious little strawberry-blonde first grader, and she was Melissa's first "regular ed" friend. Melissa was in third grade and easily fitting in with this group of young swimmers. By this stage, her social circle had widened. She wasn't shy about meeting new people and was always first through the door at the Y, greeting everyone at the front desk with a broad smile, and a "Hi!" as she made her way to the pool area. It was such a sweet feeling following her down the hall as she dragged her gym bag to the locker room. She was happy and confident. But that happiness and confidence was about to fade. Which is why I ended up really hating her fourth-grade year.

It began the day before school even started. The school invited parents of the special education kids to check out their classrooms and meet their teachers at yet another new school (Melissa's fourth). I was talking to a mother of twin girls as we walked into the lobby. A teacher directed us to a corridor on the left. We both stopped short. Above the corridor was a banner welcoming the students. The words were something like, "Welcome to our Special Students." This formidable woman, whom I would soon come to know, and who had the biggest heart, but who also didn't mince or mind her words, looked at me and said, "What stupid-ass person put that up? Ohhh, that's coming down. Do they think the parents are stupid?" She was half-laughing, but I recognized her pain immediately. In this school, which housed fourth and fifth graders, all the resource rooms were in one particular corridor. The other schools in town had interspersed the resource rooms, and there was no sense of being apart or "special." The vibe of this school felt noticeably different, and that sign represented everything we resented. We didn't want sympathy, empathy, or worse—condescension—we wanted inclusion. Special van, special entrance, special education, special kid. "Blech!" The perfect setup to ostracize a child.

It took a few days, but the sign came down because of the demands of that determined mother. But there were other signs of "specialness." Melissa's resource room had no desks in a row, and in their place was a cluster of round tables and chairs. It resembled her pre-kindergarten classroom. No other classrooms in that school of fourth and fifth graders had tables in circles. She was in the fourth grade, for Pete's sake! She had an older, very kind, and patient resource room teacher, but to me, the teacher seemed more like a sweet grandmother than a teacher with high expectations for her students. (It could be my imagination, but I swear I remember her wearing an apron the first time I saw her in the classroom.) We didn't want Melissa coddled. We wanted her to learn to read, do simple math, maybe even write, or print a simple sentence without assistance. We wanted her exposed to history and current events, and to learn about other cultures, countries, people, etc. In short, we wanted her teachers to help her achieve as much as she could.

That fall, Melissa brought home a note about a Halloween parade. Her class would be dressing up as pirates on Halloween and visiting the other classrooms.

"So, you're supposed to dress up as a pirate and visit the other classrooms?"

"Yeah," Melissa replied.

"Are you going to visit your homeroom class?"

"Uh-huh."

"Are you going to visit other classrooms?"

"Yup, fifth grade too."

"Are the other classes going to dress up too?"

"Nope, just the resource room," Melissa replied.

Jack and I exchanged glances. We dropped the discussion with her, but later that evening, we vented our anger to each other.

"What are they trying to accomplish?" Jack said indignantly.

"If all the other kids are doing this, then that's great, but singling out the resource-room kids! That's so wrong!"

"I know," I said.

"And every kid in the resource room is assigned to a regular homeroom. That means that the kid who spends fifteen minutes each morning in a homeroom and then disappears somewhere is now returning in a parade with all the resource-room kids—all the 'special' kids. Melissa may have disabilities, but she certainly knows when she's being treated like a small child and being stigmatized. She's eleven years old, for crying out loud."

"How do they expect the parents to feel about this?" Jack said. "They don't even realize how offensive and hurtful this is."

We spent a fair amount of time that evening working ourselves into a snit. It probably was more of my snit. Jack's MO was to have a short vent—and then do something. Rehashing the slights felt cathartic for the moment, but we had to respond. Jack wrote the following letter:

Oct. 4, 1988,

Dear Mrs. (Resource Room Teacher),

I understand that there are plans to have the special education students dress up as pirates on Halloween. While this sounds like fun, it is our feeling that Melissa should really participate in whatever activity Mrs. (Homeroom Teacher) has planned for this day.

Our principal concerns are that first, the "pirate" activity will tend to spotlight those students in special education; and second, it takes time away from the education assistance Melissa needs. It is our feeling that the more Melissa is integrated into the general activities of her homeroom, the less socialization will be a problem. At the same time it will give you more opportunity to focus on the special help she requires. Clearly, this is your professional strength and Melissa's greatest need.

I would appreciate it if you would share our thoughts with Mrs. (Homeroom Teacher) and advise her to let us know if Melissa needs to prepare anything for the 31st. Thank you for your support and understanding.

Sincerely,

Jack and Kathleen Tumminello

Melissa's resource room had a Halloween party, like all the other classrooms. There was no parade.

On paper, Melissa's Individual Education Plan, IEP, contained all the usual goals, but it was the non-tangible "feel" of this school that worried us. The cumulative effect of going to a new school almost every year was becoming evident. All the children in our town went to schools within their district. They took the school bus and progressed from elementary to middle, and then to high school with the same group of kids and friends.

For special education students, it was very different. They went to the school wherever the resource room was, and it varied from year to year. If the resource room for your child's grade was not in your district, your child went by van to another district. Melissa had just spent two productive years in her neighborhood school, taking the school bus with some kids she got to know who lived on our street. Now she was back to taking the van, which discharged and picked up students at the back of this new school. The kids in grades four and five already knew one another. How did anyone expect them to welcome at lunch or recess a special ed kid who they only saw in their homeroom for fifteen minutes at the beginning of the day and who then went to that resource room? Kids can be cruel, and to be fair to them, the special education kids *were* different. In this school, and because of this system, we felt our children were becoming more segregated. Children's cruelty to each other can be overlooked in that environment. It was the unintended consequence of resource rooms.

At Melissa's previous schools, if I had been attending a meeting or picking her up for a doctor's appointment after school, etc., I might see her at recess or at the end of the day interacting with other classmates. She had always appeared happy. One day, at this new school, when I was walking toward the entrance to attend a meeting, I heard the usual cacophonous din of school recess and happened to spot Melissa. She was standing apart from everyone and looked distressed. When she got home from school, I asked her about recess.

"I saw you at recess today. You looked sad. What was the matter?"

"Nobody will play with me."

"Aren't there any of your resource-room friends at recess?"

"No, they're in the other homerooms and they have recess at a different time."

"So, what do you do?"

"I just stand there."

"Every day?"

"Yeah."

"Do your resource-room friends have any friends in their homerooms?"

"No, I don't think so."

I made an appointment to talk to the principal to express our disappointment with Melissa's educational settings. She was new to the position, and I wanted her to understand our feeling that Melissa was in a more restrictive and segregated environment than she had been for the previous two years.

The principal welcomed me, and we both sat down. The meeting got off to a poor start. I started to explain what I thought the problem was: "Melissa's not her usual bubbly self this year. She's the only resource-room child in her homeroom, and she eats lunch by herself and has no one to play with at recess." The principal didn't seem to be interested in the social or emotional issues. I wanted her to at least listen to my argument that socialization was just as important as the other classroom skills Melissa was learning. She wanted me to give her other specific examples of problems. She was asking me questions like, "Is there something that you think needs to be changed on her IEP? Is there a teacher you're having a particular problem with?" She wanted concrete examples of some *thing*, some *person*, or some *issue*. Her focus was only on the curricula. Then she pointed out that class schedules could not be changed. "Is there anything else?" I felt as if I had failed to get her to see my point of view. My mind was in overdrive. All my feelings suddenly felt like a child whining, "It's not fair!" I could feel my throat tightening and eyes watering. I was overwhelmed with frustration. The principal was defending her teachers, but besides the banner in the hall, which she admitted had probably not been appropriate, there was nothing that anyone had done wrong. But it was ALL wrong in my eyes. I broke down in tears, not able to further articulate what exactly we needed and how I felt.

I later realized I should never have asked for that meeting. What I wanted was something beyond what the principal could give me. I was looking for understanding, tolerance, acceptance—*inclusion*. I wanted those qualities to be part of the fabric of that school. Inclusion was not something parents brought up with teachers. We wanted it so badly, but it seemed to be an elusive hope, a desire, and to some, even a fantasy or pipe dream. There was a clause in every IEP that explained the "criteria for movement to a less restrictive category," which was: "When the student is able to perform more appropriately with less specialized instruction, as determined by the Evaluation Team." This caveat was on every child's IEP. It was a sentence that never read true for me. It seemed to put all the onus on the child. Even the terminology was wrong in my eyes. "Less restrictive" to me implied a hindrance, an impediment—to what? Being with other children?

I didn't know this principal, and I could clearly see that she couldn't truly see my pain. I wanted her to hear me. I wanted her to understand my discomfort and sadness. I wanted her to make it better. In that principal's office I was reduced to being a small, solitary person, stamping my foot, making pathetic, inarticulate stabs for change.

There's No Special Ed Line at McDonald's

Sometimes, to fix a problem, you need a team. I became involved with a small group of parents of special education students that year. We got to know each other through our town's newly formed Special Education Parent Advisory Council, SPED PAC. A 1986 federal requirement had mandated that all public schools have one to provide parents of special education children with a voice. The PACS were to be subcommittees of public-school committees.

As with most organizations, the most active members are the ones committed to the mission. Our SPED PAC was no exception. These parents all shared a common goal: to have their children reach their maximum abilities physically, socially, and emotionally in the least restrictive environment possible. Their dream was to have their children attend an "integrated" classroom, i.e., a regular classroom that provided support services, which is what "least restricted" meant to us. Integrated classrooms were not something Massachusetts schools had in

1988, but we wanted it badly. We had all experienced seeing our children shunned. That was the year this group of parents became energized. It began with an almost-universal feeling of exclusion.

Years earlier, when Jack and I had attended a meeting for the parents of special education students to explain an Individualized Educational Plan, IEP, Jack had asked a question on our quiet ride home. "Do you think those parents were thinking about anything beyond next year?"

"Probably not," I said. "The IEP is only for a single school year."

"I understand," Jack said. "But how can they focus on short-term goals if they're not thinking about long-term ones?"

He was right. We wanted to know what was down the road. What would Melissa's future look like? Would she ever learn to read or write? Were there other children in the school system with similar disabilities? Would she graduate from high school? Surely there were children older than Melissa in special education classes, right? How were they doing? We had asked those questions at almost every meeting. We never got answers because Melissa was in one of the first official special education resource classes in our town. The Education for All Handicapped Children Act had only become a national law in 1975—five years before Melissa entered nursery school. She was part of the vanguard of special education in Chelmsford… and, in fact, the country. There were no parent groups in the school system that we could look to for answers or guidance. *We* were the trailblazers, whether we wanted to be or not.

These involved parents were looking beyond the present school year. They were looking at their child's future. One day

I commented to a SPED PAC mother about how cute her little boy with Down Syndrome was; she said to me, "Yes, he's adorable now, but he's not going to be adorable when he grows up." That comment was the crux of the challenge. As parents, we needed to be planning for adult life, and this group understood that. As I had said many times to parents, "Remember, there's no 'special ed' line at McDonald's." There was a silent undertow of apprehension in this group. Where would their child fit in society? Would society see them as individuals—separate from the disability that defined them? How would they live and maybe work in this society? Would society be ready to see and make room for them, and more importantly—accept them?

It never hurts to think big and seek out your strongest advocate if you want your issues addressed. The following year, I was a co-chair of our town's SPED PAC, and before our first planning meeting, Jack said to me, "Why not invite the Secretary of Education to Chelmsford?"

"You mean *the* Secretary of Education?" I said.

"Sure, why not? Aim high."

The PAC board composed a letter and mailed it off to the US Secretary of Education hoping it would get read. That fall we conducted a survey, and the top two issues that parents wanted us to work on were socialization and integration. Not only did we want our children mainstreamed as much as possible in school, but we also wanted our children (and the parents too) to feel they belonged to their community, their town. To our amazement, our letter was read, and passed on to the US Assistant Secretary of Education, Office of Special Education and Rehabilitative Services, who accepted our invitation. The Assistant Secretary replied he would bring his aide along... because he was deaf.

Dr. Robert Davila's acceptance of our invitation energized us. We felt his visit would give us the visibility, credibility, and respectability that we were looking for, and we needed to make this visit memorable. "Disability Awareness Week" became our campaign. The goal was to provide, to as many townspeople as possible, the educational resources to encourage social awareness of, and sensitivity to, people with disabilities. We wanted to touch every child in the school system, so we planned events at the elementary schools, middle school, and high school. The board also made sure everyone in town knew about this week.

Life gave us a gift that year—the Americans with Disabilities Act, ADA. It was a bill that addressed workplace, transportation, and housing issues and accessibility for individuals with disabilities. There was now a national conversation around disability, and we were part of it. Countless advocates, activists, and most importantly, individuals with disabilities had fought a long, hard fight, trying to give visibility to everything that had been denied to them. In fact, it wasn't so much that they had been denied, but that they had hardly been considered. They were invisible. Individuals with disabilities and their advocates weren't asking anymore; they were demanding society see and include them. We added our voices to their demands.

Of course, with change comes all the usual concerns and fears. To prepare for our big week, I got myself invited to one of the scheduled ecumenical meetings of the pastors, priests, and a rabbi in our town, and they agreed to talk about inclusion and respect for individuals with disabilities during their sermons that week. After the meeting, one priest in our former parish—the same parish that wouldn't allow Melissa to attend CCD classes—came up to me and said, "I'm so glad your request was about sermons. I thought you might be some kind of activist, wanting to talk about installing handicap ramps in all the churches." I wanted to...but that was another fight. *But why did I have to be an "activist," and why did installing a ramp have to be a "fight"?*

Dr. Davila's visit culminated with his address to the townspeople that evening at the senior citizen center, which was covered by our town's cable news channel. Our children were too young to see him as a role model, but he was the perfect embodiment of our campaign's goal, the perfect example for the townspeople to see what a person with a disability could achieve. The night before his speech, Jack and I had hosted a dinner party for the PAC board officers and our guest of honor, Dr. Davila. He told us he had accepted our invitation because he was deeply interested in hearing from parents and caregivers. Dr. Davila (who was an excellent lipreader) said he wanted to hear about our efforts, fears, concerns, and accomplishments. It was the first time I ever heard someone say they wanted to know what the parents or caregivers needed or wanted from the school system. He was listening to us, and we weren't hearing any "yes...buts." Dr. Davila heard our pleas for inclusion, and our fears for life beyond high school. He made us feel things were not impossible. Things would change. We could dare to dream of a better world for our children, but it would involve work. He shared a personal story explaining that his assistant would listen to his public speeches, and afterward, they would work on any words where he was dropping the final consonant sounds to assure that his speaking would continue to be understandable to the public. "I know the lifelong efforts a disability demands," he told us.

Our SPED PAC got the town talking about disabilities—and in a good way. There were letters of praise and recognition all around town for the SPED PAC's accomplishments that week. Our children were being recognized for who they were, part of the community. They were no longer invisible. There was a feeling that change was coming. A fruitful outcome that spring, due to the work of one parent—the one who had also got the "Welcome Special Students" banner removed—was the town's very first disability baseball team. Initially we were refused permission to use one of the baseball fields because of the fear that wheelchair tires would ruin the ball field. That argument became both outrageous and silly after our town-wide disability-awareness blitzkrieg. Although she played in a few games, Melissa wasn't all that interested in playing ball. She just wanted to swim.

Toward Independence

What Jack and I had wanted so badly suddenly happened: mainstreaming. It was no longer a dream. In the fall of 1990, Melissa's sixth-grade class at the middle school would start the program. It was the only mainstream grade in the school system; the first class of this type in Chelmsford and, in fact, one of the first in the entire state. Mainstreaming was to start small, with just the sixth grade. It was a huge shift, and as expected, the decision wasn't met with full enthusiasm or approval from some teachers. It also started to give me a "be careful what you wish for" feeling. I was reassured to hear that the regular education teachers who were open to the changes were the ones who had been selected for Melissa's classes. However, I was nervous about what regular ed classes were going to be like. This is when I did something a bit nutty. I asked if I could shadow Melissa for a day, sitting in the back of the room to observe. They let me do it.

My fears were assuaged. The teachers made the subjects interesting, the kids seemed to be their usual selves, and Melissa was just fine. She understood most of what was being taught, and the aide could break the subject down for her in the resource room, if necessary. But I had an interesting observation that day. Melissa's last class of the day was music. This teacher was exceptional. He had a passion for music, he was dynamic, and he made the class exciting—peppering the kids with questions that they all seemed eager to answer. Melissa sat in the middle of the room, and I sat in the back, surrounded by a group of girls. When the teacher started asking questions, Melissa remained quiet, but the rest of the room erupted with raised hands and kids leaning forward on their desks and half standing. Then I heard a girl murmur "ohooh" and sit heavily back down in her seat. She looked frustrated. That's when I shifted my attention to the girls sitting around me.

Since it was the end of the school day, I had time to chat with the music teacher after his class. I thanked him for indulging me and complimented him on his class. Then I told him what I had noticed. He was genuinely surprised and intent on changing. He had no idea he hadn't called on a single girl to answer any question during his class.

Melissa rarely picked up on social snubs and, looking back, I don't think she particularly cared. She had signed up for Girl Scouts after a resource room friend had invited her to join her troop. At Christmastime, they'd had a gift-swap party at the troop leader's house, and each girl brought a present for the girl whose name they had drawn the week before. As soon as I pulled my car into the driveway to pick Melissa up after the party, the troop leader ran out to the car.

"Hi, I wanted to talk to you before Melissa comes out. Ah…I feel really bad about this, umm, Melissa got a gift that is not that great."

"Why, what did she get?" I asked.

"I'm so, so sorry, umm, she got a packet of panties."

She said it so fast that my mind couldn't make sense of what she was trying to tell me. I was trying to put what she was saying into some kind of context. Panties? Did I hear her right? But before I could ask another question, the troop leader said, "The package was torn open. There were supposed to be three panties, but there were only two pairs in the package."

We both looked at each other in silence.

"I better get inside. I'll tell Melissa you're here."

Before I could think of what I would say to Melissa, she ran out and hopped into the back seat. She threw her "gift," still in the torn Christmas giftwrap, across the seat and leaned over the front seat to show me the goodie bag of cookies, candies, and Christmas trinkets she got. She was all excited and was taking everything out to show me. I backed out of the driveway and almost laughed out loud. It is a scene most parents are familiar with; a child rips open a gift, discovers it's clothing, and tosses it aside, hoping the next present will be a toy. Melissa never gave that miserable gift a second look or thought. Christmas was coming in a few days' time, and she didn't care. I was thankful I didn't have to discuss the insult with her. But as a parent…? It never seemed to end.

Jason, cut it out! Mommm, tell 'em to stop teasing me!"

While she was not always able to stand up to Jason's relentless teasing, Melissa was displaying an inner fearless integrity. Because the middle school was a central school, and special education students entering grade six from all the district elementary schools attended this one school, it was the first time in Melissa's schooling that she had a group of resource room friends: five girls, all with different abilities, disabilities, and social skills. (She attended the resource room for math and reading.) Phone calls quickly became the girls' biggest pastime. They were just now learning the skills that most children begin to deal with in the primary grades: skills such as how to get along with one another, understand another person's point of view, and have empathy.

Melissa often overreacted if any of her friends said mean things to her, or what she perceived as mean things. She also didn't understand that her words could be hurtful, too. There was no subtlety or nuance with Melissa's language. As she had limited expressive ability, if Melissa were arguing with someone, she would usually blurt out what was bothering her the most because she was trying not to forget what she wanted to say, which consequently came across as cruel, or else like a complete non-sequitur that the "culprit" somehow had to interpret. For instance, if one girl said to another that Melissa only had three friends a few days earlier, and if that girl called her on the phone, Melissa would bluntly say, "I have five, and I hate you!"

But there was one time when Melissa was angry about a quarrel between two friends, whom I shall call Rebecca and Amy, and had complete control of her responses: I was in the kitchen making dinner and Melissa was talking on the phone upstairs.

"Fine!" I heard her yell. Then she came stomping down the stairs.

The phone rang in the kitchen, and Melissa picked it up.

"I hate you too," she said then hung up.

"Melissa, what's going on?"

"Rebecca and I had a fight at lunchtime."

"About what?"

"Rebecca was making fun of the way Amy looked and didn't want her to sit with us. I was mad, so I said…so I said…so I said, 'Knock it off, she can't help the way she looks, it's just the way she is.' Then Rebecca said…she said…'Go sit with your Down Syndrome friend, then.'"

"What did you do?"

"I went and sat with Amy."

"What did the others do?"

"They sat with Amy too."

The girls hurt each other's feelings and claimed to have ended friendships almost daily; however, as much as they squabbled, they stuck together. Without regular peers for friends, they didn't want to join the other kids at lunch. But now the choice belonged to them. Ironically, it was mainstreaming that gave them the freedom to self-isolate their little lunch group. They didn't have to explain their disability to anyone…or suffer the eye rolls. They could just be themselves.

Swimming with the Sharks

Unlike Melissa's self-isolating lunch crowd, Jason had never worried about the ability to be himself. He wasn't concerned about other peoples' opinions and at times, their feelings. High school work came easily for him. He was always in bed by nine, with homework completed—except for any outlines his English teachers demanded for writing assignments. He didn't want to do them, and for the most part, he didn't do them—considering them a waste of time. I spied a composition paper he had turned in once. The grade A was crossed out; under it was a B, along with the teacher's notation, "no outline turned in." That was an acceptable tradeoff as far as Jason was concerned. It had infuriated me and his teachers, but that's how he operated. He weighed the gains and losses, pros and cons, and made his decisions—matter of fact, no hesitation.

When he was a freshman at the same Catholic high school Matthew had attended, Jason had joined the debate club. Jack had a business book at home with the ungodly long title, *Swim with the Sharks without Being Eaten Alive: Outsell, Outmanage, Outmotivate, and Outnegotiate Your Competition*. Jason had found it and read it cover to cover. That was the last of us ever winning an argument with him. He was a good debater, and he told me one day that his coach had said, "Jason, the object is to win the debate, not destroy your opponent."

One look at his bedroom left no doubt that music remained a constant in Jason's life. It was cluttered with musical instruments and equipment: keyboard, saxophone, multiple types of guitars—electric and acoustic—amps, headphones, tape players, spaghetti-like piles of cords, and a wall lined with tape cassettes with genres ranging from Mozart to Metallica.

He had left a Guns N' Roses cassette tape on the kitchen table one day, and since I had never been able to make out any of the lyrics in a heavy metal song, I took out the cover, sat down, and read them. I was appalled at the racist and misogynistic themes and promptly threw the tape in the trash. When Jason got home, I confronted him.

"You threw out my tape?"

"Yes. I read the lyrics to some of those songs, and they're trash, pure trash."

"What are you talking about?"

"They're hateful, offensive, vile…"

"So? I didn't buy it for the lyrics; I bought it for the music. I'll just buy another one."

"Oh no you won't."

Jason slammed his hand on the table. "That's stupid." He stood up, nearly knocking the chair over, and stormed up to his bedroom and slammed the door.

The argument continued at dinnertime.

"…and I'm throwing out all your Metallica and Guns N' Roses t-shirts, and any other black ones you have."

Jason became irate and I remember yelling back to him, "Don't talk to your mother like that!" I turned to Jack and said, "Are you going to let him talk to me like that?" Jason got up to leave and made another flippant remark as he walked by my chair. I jumped up and followed him, but Jack stood in the doorway and stopped me.

"Why aren't you helping me? Why are you letting him talk to me like that?"

"Hey, stop this. He's okay."

"No, he's not! He's going to end up a juvenile delinquent or in jail if this doesn't stop. All this heavy metal stuff is having a bad influence on him."

"You're overreacting; calm down."

"I'm not overreacting! I'm scared."

I knew that if Jason thought a rule was illogical, or at least didn't make sense to him, he'd either ignore it or rebel against it, and his defiance could be formidable, and we'd have a hard time fighting him.

That night I was still angry, but more so at Jack because I felt he wasn't standing up for me. Then he told me a story about a guy he knew. The fellow and his wife had about fifteen kids; some were foster care kids, and some of them could have been adopted or biological, he didn't know, but Jack said that the couple were very strict Catholics and expected the kids to follow all the church's rules as well as the house rules, period, no exceptions—one size fits all. When Jack finished his story, he said, "Do you know what they're doing right now? They're trying to find one of their teenagers who has run away. You're going to have to pick your battles with Jason." When he said that, I realized I had overreacted. I hadn't given Jason time to talk things over. He had a knack for "pushing my buttons," which invariably led to a knee-jerk reaction in me to issue orders that I thought should be followed without question because…what? I knew better, or because I said so?

I was expecting a prolonged battle over the Guns N' Roses tape, but Jason had moved on. He didn't think the argument was worth fighting about, and although he continued to grouse about the black t-shirts, it wasn't in his nature to sulk or hold grudges, so we had no further arguments about the music. I had made my feelings and opinions of the genre dramatically clear.

 One day when I had picked him up after high school band practice, he got into the car, threw his backpack on the floor, and popped a tape into the cassette player. "Listen to this," he said. It was a furiously fast and frenetic electric guitar track. "That's Joe Satriani. He's awesome. His techniques are incredible. Hear how clean and tight his music is? He's a musician's musician." For the entire ride home that day and several days afterward, he tutored me on the details of guitar playing and gave me a lifelong appreciation for near-genius-level rock-guitar-playing techniques. Years later, I brought up the Guns N' Roses incident and he said, "I thought you were being so ridiculous that day. I bought that tape for the notes, not the words."

Beyond Acceptance

Jason was doing well in school, and mainstreaming was working out for Melissa, but something was very wrong in Matthew's life. He loved his years at George Washington University and had a great group of friends. He was six foot tall, and had brown hair, hazel eyes, and a trim build. He was kind, gregarious, good looking, and the girls loved him. But now, a year after graduation, he had a job he hated, hostile new roommates, and a paycheck that was not covering his expenses. When he called home, we could hear the sadness and flatness in his voice. "How can we help you, Matthew?" we asked every time he called. All he ever said was: "You can't help me. I have to do this myself." Jack offered to connect him with associates who might get him interviews for better jobs, but Matthew rebuffed them all. It seemed like he was "spinning his wheels" and couldn't move on with his new life or career.

He had come home for Thanksgiving that year in 1991. And the day after, Melissa matter-of-factly mentioned to us, "Matt's gonna talk to you later." We thought it might be something about his job. Maybe he would move to the Boston area. That evening he came into our bedroom, turned off the TV, and sat down on a chair facing the foot of our bed. We moved to the end of the bed facing him, knees almost touching. With a lowered head and with a cracking voice that was stifling a cry, he said, "Mom, Dad, you know I've been unhappy, and I've told you that you couldn't help me, ummm…well, I've been going to a therapist to figure out just who I am, and…I'm gay." There. He got it out…It was his moment of terror.

Family was everything to Matthew. His friends knew that, and that's why the phone had been persistently ringing over that weekend. "Are you okay, Matt? Are your parents okay?" But I hadn't understood all the phone calls at that moment. Thoughts, feelings, fears: everything was swirling through my head at once. *So, this is who he is. He will never get married or have children. His life will be difficult. Questions: Big questions. Would he be safe? Would he get AIDS? Would he die?* Blurred, frantic thoughts. Time seemed to stop, but my thoughts rushed everywhere. Confused, I could hear myself, echoed by Jack to my side, telling him that we loved him and would always love him. What brought me out of my haze was Matthew's demeanor; it was what had frightened me the most when he first walked into the bedroom. Once he had said it out loud and heard us say we loved him, he let out a faint gasp—it was as if he had been holding his breath—then his shoulders relaxed, and his face immediately softened.

He told us to wait while he ran upstairs to get something. Jack and I sat there mute, barely moving. Matthew quickly returned and said, "You need to read this." He handed us the book *Beyond Acceptance: Parents of Lesbians and Gays Talk About Their Experiences.* "I underlined sections and put in my comments and thoughts. I want you to know how I feel about them." We talked further, and, smiling with relief as he left the room, he turned and said, "Well, I'm out of the 'closet,' and now you're in!"

Matthew went out with friends that night, and Jack became very unsettled. He wanted Matthew. He wanted to see him, hug him, talk to him. He was trying to process it all. Neither of us slept well, and, sometime during the night, Jack rolled over, wrapped his arms around me, and sobbed. He didn't say anything; he just sobbed. The next day, he expressed his dismay to Matthew that he had gone out with his friends instead of staying home to talk a little more with us. Matthew quickly picked up on his fear, apologized, and said, "Dad, I'm the same person today as I've been all the days before. If you loved me then, you should love me now. You're not going to lose me." It was what Jack needed to hear.

Yet maybe we had lost him in one sense. Reflecting on it, Jack and I had to ask ourselves a tough question: Had we lost sight of him while we were trying to raise Jason and Melissa? Did he get lost in the almost daily challenges? It was easy to overlook Matthew. He had never been passionate about something, like Jason was about music, or Melissa was about swimming (unless you include his excitement at watching a hurricane or winter blizzard roar through). He was a docile, kind, loving, and cooperative child. He did well in school and his teachers always praised him. He was never a problem.

We knew we had to talk to Jason to tell him about Matthew, and I assumed Jack was as worried as I was. What if Jason doesn't accept Matthew for who he is? What would it do to the family? However, we were both too afraid to vocalize it. It was probably close to the same trepidation Matthew had felt when he came out to us. We sat across from Jason at the kitchen table and told him that Matthew was gay. There wasn't much discussion, because Jason quickly said, "Mom, Dad, it's no big deal. I get it. Matt's Matt. I'm good with that."

"Surely you must have known," some of our friends said. Surely, we didn't. We really didn't. Homosexuality had not been on our radar while raising Matthew. LGBTQ+ issues are matter-of-fact topics now, but they had been taboo topics when Matthew was growing up—never mentioned, and never in our thoughts. Frankly, Jack and I were ignorant of so much. Matthew became our guide and teacher. Four weeks after he came out, when he was home again for Christmas, we asked him what we could do to help him, and he responded, "Come here." We followed him into our mudroom. "Look," he said, pointing to Jason's beat-up school loafers. "Fag" was written on the side of one loafer. It had been there for months. I looked at Matthew's face. His lips were tight, and his jaw muscles were flexing. He was so angry. How many times had Jack and I walked by those shoes and never noticed? Matthew, who was only home for the weekend, had spotted the slur immediately. That foul, dehumanizing word had been invisible to us. Matthew's life had been invisible to us. See me, love me, his eyes were screaming. He turned to us and said, "You can help me by speaking up, Mom, Dad. You can't stay silent."

We showed Jason the loafer. "This stuff hurts Matthew, Jason. You can't do this," Jack said. Jason listened in silence. Jack added, "I don't want to see or hear any more of this stuff—ever."

As evidence of my blindness to Matthew's pain—to the life he was now trying to understand and live—I found out later that the lyrics that had been so offensive to me on Jason's cassette tape had also been very homophobic. I had focused only on the sexist and racist messages. Matthew's anger in that mudroom was aimed at all of us. It wasn't enough to say we were "okay" with Matthew. We had to support and defend him.

We had never asked Jason why he had written "fag" on his shoe. We had been solely focused on the immediate need to help Matthew in any way we could, but I asked him about it recently, and he replied, "To be honest, I don't think I knew what the word meant, and if you had asked me then what it meant, I think I would have said it meant a "loser," and I just knew I didn't want to be called that."

"But Jason, you're smart, you weren't gay, and I'm sure you weren't labeling yourself as a fag, so why write it?"

"I don't remember, but it was probably an immature, junior-high-level thing guys would do. Remember that kid who played the violin who I hung around with in eighth grade? Well, one day I was over at his house and his mother started yelling, 'Get down here!' She was really, really mad. She called us downstairs and pointed to my friend's notebook. He had drawn swastikas all over the cover. His family was Jewish. He had no idea what a swastika meant. To him it was just a cool design. So, I'm guessing writing that word was a similar, stupid, immature thing that I did."

Before he left for DC, Matthew asked us, "Could you do me a favor? Could you go to some PFLAG meetings?" (PFLAG was a support group for parents and family of gay and lesbian children and adults.) We replied, "Of course, of course, we'll go." Talking to him on the phone a few weeks later, I said,

"Matthew, I'm confused about the PFLAG meetings. Just what is it you think we need help with?" I told him some parents at the meetings were stuck on the same issues week after week. "They're afraid to tell their families and friends that their son or daughter is gay; I get that. And they don't want to be shunned by their coworkers and friends. I get that too, but I think we're past that point, Matthew; is there something else we need to work on?" He sounded exasperated with me. "Mom," he said, "I wanted you and Dad to go to the meetings to help them! I want you to fight for me the way you fight for Melissa. It's the same struggle; respect and dignity for the person you are."

It was the same struggle, but this one was a hard climb. The AIDS epidemic was raging, and with no cure in sight, someone had to be blamed for this "plague." Fr. Byrne had died, and his message of love and acceptance had been replaced. The substitute priests' sermons no longer emphasized universal, unconditional love.

One Sunday, when the priest was railing against homosexuality yet again, tears began to well up in my eyes. My throat burned as I tamped down a sob. *This is my son you're talking about. He has no need to repent to a God who you say created him in his own image.* I didn't want anyone to see my red, watery eyes. I wanted to leave. But since we were seated so far away from the side door, I felt trapped. Parishioners faded away from my view, and it felt like that priest was looking directly into my eyes, and every word he uttered was a personal condemnation of Matthew that I had to listen to in silence. *How dare he!* I thought. This was not a message of love. To me, it was sowing seeds of hate. I walked out of our little church that

Sunday never to return. I had learned from Melissa; if she could ignore or not care about snubs, as she had at that first Girl Scout Christmas party, surely, I could walk away from this "love everyone, *except*..." philosophy.

One afternoon, Jack and I were walking along a congested sidewalk on Newbury Street in Boston. The street is lined with shops, cafes, and restaurants, and draws a lot of shoppers, tourists, and students from nearby colleges and universities. We heard two males behind us talking and laughing about "fags," "homos," etc. Jack and I exchanged glances. My rushed thoughts were: What do we do? Is this the time to speak up? What will happen if we do? Will we be accosted? Instincts prevailed, and Jack and I turned around at the same time and gave them a stern, disapproving stare. The two males were boys in their teens talking "dirt." The boy who was talking stopped mid-sentence and looked at us. The expression on his face was one of shame and embarrassment. Our stares had put them in their place. But would we have been tuned in to that kind of language just a few months earlier? Would I have been strong enough to stand up, speak up? I had my doubts.

We were becoming aware of and sensitized to the hurt and danger in Matthew's world. There were no laws protecting him. Where he lived, where he worked, who he loved, where he shopped or ate, all could be "determined" by others. Matthew had learned over the years to be super-vigilant of slurs, looks, words scrawled on books, walls, etc. He was always aware of his surroundings, noticing remarks, vibes, looks, and anything that might foretell trouble. It was a matter of self-protection and safety. They were warnings. *You don't belong here. You don't deserve to be alive.*

Talking to him one day, I said, "Matt, Dad and I feel so bad about not recognizing how unhappy you were growing up. It breaks my heart to think about how sad your childhood was."

"Mom! I had a great childhood. Taking tennis lessons, trying out for the track team, like you and Dad wanted me to do—trying to fit in, *those* were the times that terrified me—not growing up in our family. I loved home. It was the one place where I felt safe." Then, voicing a hurt, he said, "I don't want you to feel bad, but remember that bike you bought me in Paris?"

Ahh, the bike! We had bought it on that Paris trip we had taken when he was little. He had been so well behaved that Jack and I had wanted to reward him by buying him something very special and something you couldn't buy in the States. So off we went, with Matthew in tow, to Printemps department store, where we picked out *the* most nifty-difty two-wheeled bicycle we had ever seen. It was shiny blue, had handbrakes, thick, white, Michelin tires and was collapsible, and because it folded in half, it didn't have a middle bar like a boy's bike, but that hadn't bothered Jack and me, no siree. Matthew hadn't been at all excited. We had thought that was because he couldn't ride a two-wheeler yet.

By the time he was big enough to ride the bike and work the hand brakes, all the kids in the neighborhood were riding bikes that had banana seats and monkey handlebars. But not our boy. Nooo, our boy was riding a bike that was *so* much better than everyone else's. Why, clearly everyone could see there was none like it.

"Mom, I wanted the kind of bike *everybody* had, not one that *nobody* had."

"Why didn't you say anything to us?"

"I didn't want you to be ashamed of me."

"Ashamed of you? Why would we have been ashamed of you?"

"I didn't want you to feel the shame that I felt."

"Oh, Matthew, if only we could go back and fix it for you."

After Matthew told me this, I thought a lot about his pain. He was only six years old at that time. What six-year-old internalizes shame so much that he worries about bringing that shame to his parents? A shame about something he didn't understand and didn't have any words for. A shame that made him endure the daily embarrassment of riding a bicycle that made it impossible for him to feel like everybody else. He was only six, yet he already knew the world around him expected him to be different. *How does one live with that?* I thought.

Matthew and I are private people. Some of our deepest thoughts and feelings we don't share with anyone—ever. But I had persisted in wanting to know at least something about what he went through. Matthew was reluctant at first, but then, in a slightly angry tone, he said, "Do you want to know about the time a kid at school pulled a knife on me?"

My heart sank. "Oh, Matt."

"Yeah, he pulled a knife on me. I was a sophomore or junior, I don't remember, but I had lost a vocabulary book and you and Dad were angry that you had to buy another one for me. After school, one of the school bullies came over to me and pulled out a hunting knife and cut the front cover of my book in half."

"A hunting knife? Are you sure it wasn't a pocketknife or something?"

"Mom, this was New Hampshire. A lot of guys had hunting knives at school. Anyway, he says to me, 'What're you going to do about it? Huh? Huh?' He was itching for me to make a move, but I froze, and then another kid began yelling, and he stopped."

That had been a story he was willing to tell me about. The others…?

Years later, I also experienced an ugly incident: Matthew had invited me to join him for a weekend at a Florida resort where he was attending a conference. We had decided to have dinner one of the nights at a lovely, upscale Italian restaurant in town. We were dining on the outside patio facing the main street; I had my back to the street, and Matthew was opposite me. It was delightful. Suddenly, Matthew stopped mid-sentence and looked beyond me with a look of fear on his face. I heard a commotion and turned around just in time to see a pickup truck going by with a large American flag waving from the bed of the truck, and two guys leaning out and screaming something. It happened so fast. I turned back to Matthew, who was sitting bolt upright, and said, "What did they say?" He put his head down and mumbled something. He wasn't going to repeat what they said, but I knew, whatever it was, it was aimed at him. That tony town will always be tainted in my eyes with that scary incident.

Three Shiny Leaves

Poison ivy was a constant intruder on the family compound. No matter how carefully we weeded the gardens, or how often we mowed the grass, the lurking root system would throw up its ubiquitous tendrils. The first signs of a shiny, green, three-leafed vine that would snake along the ground or climb anything in its path, including the apple trees, were tiny reddish leaves on thin vines poking up through the grass or flowerbeds. Growing up, there were parts of the property that were mostly off-limits for playing or walking barefoot. These were the tall grasses near the apple trees and the land that stretched to the L-shaped stone walls defining two sides of our property. My father's solution had been to mow all the cleared land constantly. My solution had been to avoid the tall grasses. But, since we had built our house among the apple trees, we now had to identify and address the transgressor. Poison ivy has a telltale giveaway in the fall or winter. Unlike other weeds or vines, older poison ivy shoots can become short, woody stalks. They stick straight up like cobras, poised and ready to inflict their venom. But they are easy to grab and strong enough to offer you a chance at uprooting them.

Jack and I would spend designated fall weekends trying to eradicate them. And every year, no matter how protected

I was, in gloves, long-sleeved shirts, and socks pulled up over my pant legs, they still managed to strike, producing an oozy, red, itchy rash. Some stalks would come up easily, but pulling up one strong vine inevitably uprooted others that crisscrossed along its path, leaving a tangle of still-thriving vines behind. If we were lucky enough to uproot a very long one, it would travel deeper and become thicker the more we tugged, and when it wouldn't budge any further, we'd have to chop the thick root with a spade or small hand saw. This routine went on for several years until one chilly fall afternoon, when I was tired and holding a large piece of root that looked like a small log in my gloved hand, I had realized that the vine was not an intruder; much like the bigotry, hatred, and intolerance in the world, it had always been there. We could never eliminate it. Even the large pile of tangled vines dying on the cold ground next to me was still capable of harming with its poisonous touch. The most we could do was manage whatever evil the vine attempted to impose upon our family space.

The woods that grew at the far end of our property, marked by the shorter stone wall, contained no apple trees, so we left it in its natural wild state there—testament to our inability to eradicate its malevolence. And there, without any further resistance, it flourished with deceptively beautiful, glossy summer leaves that turned crimson-hued in the fall. And woe to anyone who was ignorant of or heedless to its toxic nature.

Reading the book that Matthew gave us, I came across a section he had underlined. He had annotated it: "Suicide is not an option, but almost every gay person considers it. I'm going to work my hardest to change this and to end needless suffering and pain." I didn't talk to Matthew directly about suicide for some time, and I know it was because I was afraid of what he might say, but eventually, I felt I had to ask: "Did you ever think about suicide, Matt?" He surprised me by immediately responding, "Yes," as if he had been waiting for the question—but then he choked up. "I couldn't do it… because I knew how it would destroy our family." Openly sobbing, and having a hard time getting the words out, he said, "…and Melissa wouldn't understand…I loved you too much to follow through with it."

One day, I was pulling up weeds under the apple tree near the old stone fireplace. The tiny weed seedlings resembled miniature apple trees: roots, main stem, and one serrated leaf on each side of the stem. When I was a child, I had thought they were apple tree seedlings and would grow into trees, but no matter how hard I had tried to protect them from my father's mowers, no tree had ever sprouted. I later realized they were ordinary nuisance weeds. Despite that, each spring I continued to search for signs of new little apple trees, confident in the belief that they would grow into a tree just like the one above.

On this hot afternoon, I sat down to rest on the stone steps under that same apple tree and looked up at Matthew's bedroom window. I thought of all the years he had slept in that room above ours, trying desperately to hide who he really was from us and from the outside world—trying to be that perfect child, invisible, and…contemplating ending it all. My eyes wandered over to the stone fireplace and to the gate of my "secret room." Even then, years later as an adult, the sight of that "room" still imbued warmth, happiness, and remembrances of childhood innocence and joy. I glanced up at Matthew's bedroom again. Such different "rooms," I think.

On October 9, 1992, 12,000 quilts were spread out on the National Mall in Washington, DC. It was the first installation of the AIDS Quilt Names Project. Seeing the media coverage of the event brought to mind a powerful and memorable scene in *Gone with the Wind,* where a frantic Scarlett is rushing to the makeshift hospital at the Atlanta rail depot to find the doctor for Melanie. The rail yard is littered with wounded Confederate soldiers. As Scarlett makes her way around stretcher-bearers and bodies in the rail yard, the camera zooms out to reveal dozens of wounded soldiers, and then zooms out again to reveal hundreds and hundreds of wounded or dead soldiers, dramatically demonstrating the enormity of the casualties of war.

An aerial view of the AIDS quilt project that weekend looked like a collection of multicolored blankets covering most of the Mall's green space. It was a deceptively colorful and bucolic scene. However, the display represented only a portion of the casualties of another war. It was a war that was still raging, with no end in sight, and with no survivors. As the camera zoomed in, each square "blanket" became twenty-four quilts. The camera zoomed in again, showing groups of quilts, with the final closeup shots revealing individual quilts with names attached—sons, daughters, brothers, sisters, friends, lovers—all cherished and mourned—all representing the collected magnitude of individual losses. They were beguiling in their quiescence, each quilt a life, each quilt unique, and each quilt sewn with a silent prayer—*Remember me.*

Matthew had ripped off the opaque film covering our eyes. It hurt and stung. He made us see him clearly. His world was scary, and we couldn't protect him—only stand up for him and love him. Not surprisingly, Melissa was the first family member to give Matthew a boost of self-assurance. Matthew volunteered at the NAMES Project AIDS Memorial Quilt and because of this, he and other volunteers and organizers were invited to participate in Bill Clinton's inaugural parade. Matthew called home and invited Melissa to join him.

The weekend Matthew was planning was, to use his words, "a big gay weekend." They went to a concert to hear an a-cappella group, The Flirtations, which Melissa loved. (The Flirtations sang over-the-top campy songs, some of which celebrated the gay community and culture.) Remembering the weekend, Matt told me, "I watched her as she laughed and laughed. It wasn't straight fun, or gay fun. To Melissa, it was just fun. Melissa sees life as it should be; she never gives it a label." Matthew later told me, "Melissa's visit made me more okay."

Fulfilling a Dream

Despite that first Christmas party, Girl Scouts worked out for Melissa. She enjoyed scouting, the field trips, activities, winter camping, and swimming: she loved it all. I didn't realize it, but Girl Scouts underscored a trait in Melissa I didn't appreciate; her determination to set personal goals and reach them. Her scouting projects were of her choosing, and within her abilities. She saw all the badges proudly displayed on her sash as visible signs of her accomplishments. I don't think she even thought about the possibility of not trying to achieve a Silver and Gold Award—the two highest Girl Scout Awards—which she attained. But swimming was Melissa's first love, and, after four years of lessons, she, along with her friend Kelly, signed up for the Y's newly formed swim team, the "Sting Rays," to learn the basics of swim team competition.

"I'm ready," she yelled. It was her first day of practice, and she was holding the back door open, eager to get to the Y.

"Wait, wait," I called out. "Do you have everything in your bag? Check it," I said. "Make sure you've got the Speedo bathing suit, and goggles and swim cap."

"I already did," she groaned.

"Okay, let's go."

She slung her bag over her shoulder, and we headed for the

car. Backing out of the garage, I said, "Okay, now what are you going to do when you're on the starting block?"

"Don't look at you?"

"Right."

We laughed. It was a problem because if Melissa made eye contact with me, she'd start giggling and lose her concentration. She wanted to compete and win, but mostly she wanted to have fun. Watching her from behind the steamy plexiglass window in the observation room during her practices, I could see that she was never first off the block—most of the time she was a good second or two behind. Even so, when the Sting Rays competed with other YMCAs in the greater Boston area, Melissa won a good number of meets in her class. She never got off the block as soon as the signal was given, but when she surfaced, her strong arm and shoulder muscles pulled her forward with forceful strokes, and you could hear the low, sonorous "thruuump" when she kicked her legs. With each stroke, she gained a little on her opponent. Her underwater turns were also powerful, helping her keep her edge. Noticeably, she had one style and speed. It was regular and powerful, and no amount of cheering or yelling could make her go faster. All her wins—every one of them—were "a come-from-behind win."

After two years, some swimmers were talking about trying out for their high school swim teams, and Melissa wanted to do the same. Her coach thought she had the strength and skills to do it. I already knew she had the strength. Each year she took part in the swim team's fundraising swim-a-thon. Two hundred laps, nonstop, two hours, 6.2 miles. There was no question of her strength or endurance.

"Let's not mention your disabilities, Melissa; let the high school coach judge you on your swimming abilities, just like the other girls."

I drove Melissa to the first tryout practice for the high school team. It was at a swimming-and-tennis club near our home. As she got out of the car, she turned back and asked, "Are you going to stay, Mom?"

"Do you want me to?"

"Yeah, but you don't have to stay the whole time."

I knew Melissa was nervous, so I stayed. It was early morning and there were only a few adults and some staff members in the pool area when we walked in. I took a chaise lounge and tried to look nonchalant and uninterested—as if I were enjoying the morning sun. When the girls began swimming, I could see that Melissa was holding her own. She had strong strokes and turns, and I noticed she was a better swimmer than a couple of the girls.

At the next practice, I saw the coach bring out a large, square, brown-and-white timer-clock and place it near the edge of the pool. It had a hand that measured a minute in five-second intervals. I lowered the book I was "reading" and sat up straight to listen. The coach wanted each swimmer to dive into the pool and do a lap at fifteen-second intervals. One swimmer would dive in and start swimming, then the next girl would dive fifteen seconds later, making for a continuous loop of swimmers in various lanes at evenly spaced intervals. I watched as Melissa approached the pool edge. I saw her eyes widen, and just as she glanced over at me with the look that usually meant, *What do I do now?* The coach yelled, "Go!" and she dove into the pool.

I knew what was wrong. Melissa couldn't figure out the fifteen-second timing. The part of her brain that deals with space, time, and math didn't function well at all. Melissa didn't want to tell the coach about her disability, and neither did I. After that practice, we went home and practiced over and over, counting by five and starting the count from anywhere on the sixty-second timer clock. She practiced for days. I could see the slight hesitation in her dives at the fifteen-second mark, but I wasn't sure if anyone else detected it. By the end of that summer, she had earned her spot on the team.

Melissa was the overachiever in the family. Making the high school JV swim team had not only been a goal she had set for herself, but she had known it carried responsibility as well—much like her Girl Scout badges. One afternoon, before I left for work (I had returned to nursing full-time), I had dropped her off for a swim meet at the Y. Jack was to pick her up. That night when Melissa had gone to bed, Jack started laughing and said, "Melissa called me from a payphone after the meet. She wasn't at the Y."

"Oh my God, where was she?"

"At Lowell High School."

"But she told me…? How the heck did she get there?"

"She thought the meet was supposed to be at the Y, but it was at the high school. She couldn't call you, so she went up to the front desk and explained the situation. They called her a taxi and paid for the trip across town. She didn't have enough time to change, so she got into the cab— in her bathing suit and swim cap."

Near the end of Melissa's second swim season, I got a call from her coach who, by now, was aware of Melissa's weaknesses, as were the girls. The coach said there was a girl who would enter school the following year who was a dynamo swimmer, and it looked like Melissa would be cut from the team. The coach wanted me to be warned in advance. She didn't want Melissa to be surprised or hurt. I understood and told her I appreciated her concern and was thankful for the call. I talked to Melissa about it, and she was okay with calling it quits. It surprised me and I asked her why she wasn't upset.

"The coach is always yelling 'go, go, faster, faster,' when I swim, and I don't like it."

"Does she do that to everyone?"

"Yeah, but she does it more to me, and I don't like it when she yells."

I tried to make her feel better. "Doesn't she know you only have one speed?" I said with a laugh.

The call from Melissa's coach happened right before her last meet, and since she would not be taking part in the regional championship meets, I knew this would be her final time swimming with the team. It was a cold winter night, and the evening sky was already losing its light when we pulled into the parking lot next to the gym. Melissa found the locker room, and I found an empty space to sit at the end of a bleacher. Because I was working, I couldn't watch any of Melissa's high school meets, and, as a result I didn't know any of the parents. I wasn't even sure if I was sitting on the "visitor" or "home" team side.

Finally, both teams came out of the locker room, and the usual cheers erupted. I quickly realized I was sitting on the "visitors" side. The team captain gathered her teammates around for their ritual chant. Melissa looked serious, maybe even nervous. The coach was holding her clipboard and probably making sure swimmers were at their posts when their race came up, and scores and times were recorded, etc. I didn't know what the roster or race sequence looked like, or even really understand the rules of the swim meet, so I just kept my eyes on Melissa. A whistle blew and the first set of girls from both teams positioned themselves on the blocks for the first race. The whistle blew again, and off they shot. Cheers and rhythmic shouts of "go, go, go," reverberated off the ceramic-tiled walls. Still watching Melissa, I saw the coach gesture for her to get ready to take her position at the block. She adjusted her goggles, tugged up her swimsuit at the shoulders, pulled down around the leg openings, and stepped onto the block. The whistle blew, and she dove in. I cheered and yelled along with the crowd. (It was weird, knowing that the people around me assumed I was cheering for Melissa's opponent.) The race was fifty meters freestyle—three sets of swimmers from each school. Until the last swimmer finished, the times were not known, so the winners of their categories are not immediately evident.

Melissa's last race was a medley relay; it's the race that gets the entire gallery on its feet. It's the race that ends the meet. You don't have to wait for the timekeeper to figure out the winner; it's obvious. The girls were adjusting their caps and goggles and getting into position. There were two blocks, two teams, four girls on each relay team. One started on each block, with their participating team members lined up behind. *Tweeeeeet!* The deafening sound of the whistle and the crowd's roar ricocheted off the blue-tiled surfaces. The swimmers shot off the blocks, down the length, turned, and aimed for the far end. Some of the girls followed them along the sides of the pool, yelling and screaming encouragements. The crowd noise reached a crescendo as each girl completed her turn and began the surge for home with the next swimmer already crouched and ready to spring.

Melissa got on the block. She was the last leg of the relay. *Could she maintain the team's lead? Would she lose time getting off the block?* The noise was so loud, my ears were ringing, and I could barely breathe in the steamy-damp chlorine air. The school teams were screeching. My heartbeat had already picked up their tempo of "Go, go, go!"

The race was tight. *Good turn, Melissa. Now keep it up.* She turned for her final lap. The other girl turned for her final lap. They were neck and neck. The noise was deafening. *Would her opponent surge and pull ahead? Could Melissa hold on?* Her strokes seemed slower than her opponent, but they were strong. I stood up. Melissa was approaching the pool wall, but I couldn't tell from where I was standing which swimmer would reach it first. Then I heard the roar—the roar from the opposite bleachers. She had done it! She brought home the win for her team. The girls were clustered in groups, hugging and high-fiving, whooping it up, looking for their parents, friends, and boyfriends in the crowd. That's when I realized I was the only one cheering for Melissa in that icy-blue-lit gym.

I looked at the spectators in the bleachers across the gym, and thought, *If only you knew what it took to get to this point; the little girl who had to think about where her feet were—yet mastered underwater turns, the little girl who couldn't use both sides of her body in unison—yet learned all the swimming strokes.*

If only you knew…

I stepped down off the riser and made my way over to Melissa, who was still in the pool. "You did it, you did it," I cried. "Here, let me take a picture." Melissa started mugging for the camera. Her coach came over and told her she also came in third in the fifty-meter freestyle—another win. It didn't seem to impress Melissa. She didn't want to race anymore; she just wanted to swim. I could hear the girls behind me making plans to meet up after the meet, so I quickly said, "Dad's going to be so proud of you. Go change. Let's go home." I've never felt so alone among so many happy, cheering people as I did that night.

The team banquet at the end of the season was more of the same. The long head table, where the team members sat, faced the parents and guests. Melissa sat on the far-right side at the end of the table. After the accolades, awards, and sport letters were distributed, small groups formed. The girls took pictures of each other and exchanged hugs. Melissa was standing in the middle of the banquet room. She was ignored. It was awkward. I wanted to scream. I leaned over to Jack, and said, "If they would just look at her and smile, for God's sakes! Include her in the group hugs!" Melissa's hurt could so easily have been avoided that night by an encouraging remark or even a simple smile—a small gesture that is so needed in the world of the disabled—heck, in anybody's world.

Looking back on Melissa's experience on the swim team, I can see she paid the price for being the first kid with significant disabilities to join the swim team (maybe even the only one to this day). But it was her dream, and she made it come true, accomplishing what she had set out to do many years before at the YMCA. The girls didn't know how to relate to her. They never knew her. But there was one girl who did know Melissa—Kelly. And Kelly was the dynamo swimmer who would take Melissa's place.

Choices

The appearance of Melissa's burns didn't bother her. She ignored the stares, but she still had a hard time explaining when asked about them. When she had been in fifth grade, she had come home one day and said, "What do I say when somebody asks me about my burns, Mom?"

"Honey, just say, 'I was burned when I was a baby.'"

"I do," she said, "but then they ask me questions."

"Well, then you can say, 'I don't remember anything about it.' That's all you need to say."

That had been the year she had her first surgery to correct the tight adhesion behind her left knee. The surgeon had to make a Z-shaped incision behind her knee to release the tight band of scar tissue. It had only involved a couple of days in the hospital. Melissa was admitted to the non-acute reconstructive surgical unit at Shriners. The unit was a large, square room with bed cubicles arranged along the walls to the left, right, and in front of the nurse's station. Each child had a designated nurse to care for them, and the layout allowed the charge nurse to see all the children at one glance. I had been waiting for Melissa to return from the recovery room when I noticed the little girl. She was about three or four years old and was sitting quietly on her bed with the safety rails up. She turned her head and looked at me. She had dark, curly hair, chubby cheeks, big, round eyes, and on each side of her small mouth was the imprint of an electrical cord—an upside-down "u," a forever frown. She won't remember the incident either, but unlike Melissa, she'll never have to explain how it happened. The burns on her mouth would tell it all.

But now, it couldn't be postponed any longer. The swim season was over, and Melissa had reached her final growth height; it was time to have the surgery to repair the deep tissue damage on her right leg. She understood the surgery she was about to have. The preparation for this surgery began weeks before Melissa was admitted. Her doctor had surgically implanted a balloon tissue-expander under the skin of her right thigh, and each week I injected a saline solution into the port on the implant until it stretched her skin to the size of a grapefruit; this would assure a sufficient amount of tissue could be stretched over the wound above her knee when the surgeon removed the thick keloid. A skin graft, to be taken from her left buttocks, would cover the wound below her right knee when the scar tissue was removed.

On the day of the surgery, as we waited for the anesthesiologist, I watched as he visited each child scheduled for surgery. There were no outbursts or crying. I think it was because of the doctor's extreme gentleness and experience with these children and maybe because of the children's own experiences with past inconceivable pain that calm prevailed. I surmised that several of the children had undergone many operations before and were veterans. The anesthesiologist was talking to a small boy who appeared to be about six or seven years old.

They were discussing what type of anesthesia the little guy wanted.

"How did you feel the last time?" the doctor asked. "Did you throw up a lot? Were you dizzy?" This child was all alone, with no parent with him. An hour later, wearing a colorful pediatric johnny covered with little animal figures and hospital-issued disposable slippers, he walked to the operating room with his nurse by his side. *How many times had he done this?* The ethos fascinated me. The nurses and doctors didn't baby their patients. They managed their pain, changed their dressings, and comforted them; however, if the children could bathe and feed themselves, then that was what was expected of them. Somehow, the children picked up on it. No one was different here. It was a shared experience. What made it work was the way the staff made every child feel they were an essential part of the team. They respected the children's wishes. They listened to them. And they empowered them.

I brushed aside the long strands of hair clinging to her damp forehead as she whimpered in discomfort. Melissa's surgery was over, and she was still groggy. She had been returned to her bed and placed on her stomach, so I had to bend down to see her face and comfort her. Her nurse watched me and said, "Don't worry, I'll make sure she's in as little pain as possible, Mom." Shriners allowed one parent to stay overnight with their child for the duration of their surgery and post-op recovery. I had stayed with Melissa. Neither Melissa nor I remember much else of those four days.

At her first follow-up visit, the nurse helped Melissa onto the examination table, and then onto her stomach. The surgeon came in and before he removed the large dressings, he said to Jack and me, "I want to warn you it's going to look bad, but it will improve in a few weeks. You can look away if you—"

"Is it going to hurt?" Melissa interrupted.

The nurse quickly jumped in and said, "No, dear, the doctor is only going to take the dressings off so he can see how you're doing."

I could already smell the iodophor-soaked gauze as the doctor pulled back the last delicate layers of gauze covering the skin graft and the tissue expansion site. The nurse in me vanished. The graft site below her knee was bright pink, which meant it was a success, but what I saw looked like a piece of raw flesh. The doctor explained that when thick scar tissue is cut into, the skin splits open, and a depression results. It was an exaggeration, but all I could think about and consequently "see" was the skin of a baked ham, splitting open when cut— with all the underlying fat exposed on both sides of the cut with the meat exposed at the bottom of the incision. I felt faint and quickly stepped out of the room on the pretext that I was going to sneeze, but I really needed to put my head down and take a deep breath. I was only gone for a moment; when I returned, Jack silently looked at me with wide eyes. He, too, was taken aback. Melissa was teary and trying to twist her body so she could see the surgical site. Thankfully, she couldn't see much. The surgeon turned to Jack and me and said, "If you want, we can do more reconstructive surgery to fill in the depression a little more," but, before we could answer, Melissa loudly and firmly said, "No more." Her decision was respected.

The Driving Test

Life outside of school was a lot kinder to Melissa. When the weather was decent, she liked to walk to our town center. It was a little over a quarter of a mile from home, all downhill. At the bottom of the hill lay the center. A brook ran horizontally under the main road, which is why that part of town seemed to be in a caldron-like setting. Beyond the brook, going uphill was the traditional white-steepled Congregational church and adjacent cemetery next to the town green, and beyond that, a cluster of other denomination churches and the fire station. In the center "bowl" were a diner, gift shop, assorted small shops, a bank, a pharmacy, two gas stations, and a supermarket.

I would often give Melissa a list of items that she could pick up for me at the pharmacy or supermarket, and sometimes give her money to buy lunch. I was taken aback one day while I was getting gas at the service station nearest our street. The attendant leaned into the car and said, "Hi Melissa!" "Hi," she shot back. How did he know her? She didn't drive. I turned to Melissa, who had a smirk on her face. The attendant laughed when he saw my reaction. "She says 'hi' to me every time she walks by. She always has a smile on her face." Jack got the same jolt one day when he went to the supermarket with her. He came home and said, "Jeez, even the deli guy knows Melissa. I stepped up to place my order, and the guy ignores me and says, 'Hi, Melissa, how are you?'" Melissa seemed to have had an organic connection with people.

Movies, malls, pizza, birthday parties, and sleepovers: all the typical teenage scenes had played out for Melissa, much like any other teenager. By her senior year, Melissa had something planned with her friends every weekend, which meant that Jack or I would have to drive her and do the drop-off, pick-up thing. Jason was attending Berklee College of Music, so he wasn't available to help with the driving. Melissa's social calendar was creeping into our free time. Dinner and a movie with Jack on the weekend meant Melissa would have to arrange transportation with one of her girlfriends (not easily done) or forgo her activity…which led to tears. It was tough to explain to her that we—Mom and Dad—had things we wanted to do. And yeah, sometimes we just wanted to spend a quiet night at home and didn't want to drive her anywhere. That's when she began to talk about getting her license, and that terrified us.

The girlfriends were always planning get-togethers that involved driving, but they didn't have their licenses either. "Why can't I get my license?" Melissa would cry, every weekend. We couldn't put off a serious discussion any longer. We didn't think Melissa was capable of driving. She had to pause to determine left from right, still had to decode some words to read them correctly, and frequently got numbers confused; Rt 95 vs. Rt 93 might look the same to her, and north and south meant nothing to her. But Melissa needed to understand the problem. She was persistent in her feeling that she could do this, so after some research, I found that with a doctor's referral and a copy of her medical records, I could have Melissa tested in the Driver Evaluation Program at a nearby rehabilitation facility.

On the day of the testing, Melissa was asked to do some simulated driving exercises. She was nervous and wanted to perform well. One testing station resembled a video game at an arcade. There was a driver's seat, steering wheel, gas, and brake pedals and a stoplight, with the obligatory red, yellow, and green lights. After the first few tests, I could see that Melissa was looking for positive feedback. Her eyes kept darting back and forth between the task at hand and the examiner. Then the tester smiled at her, and Melissa smiled back. Her shoulders relaxed, and she stopped leaning forward toward the steering wheel, which belied her attempt at concentration. She thought she was doing fine. But as I watched, I could see that the simulations were beyond her capabilities. For her sake, I wanted her to pass, but for my sake, I wanted her to fail. How cruel for both of us. We went home and waited for the results.

The evaluation determined that Melissa's braking reaction time was below the standard approved time; she had "awkward motor planning," "decreased visual convergence," "difficulty with right/left discrimination," and they recommended she see a neuro-ophthalmologist. "If she managed to get approval at that time, she could pursue her learner's permit."

The analysis told us nothing we didn't know already, and a neuro-ophthalmologist would not be able to correct the problem. But now it was Melissa who understood and accepted her weaknesses. She reluctantly agreed that driving would be impossible, but we still had that problem of transportation.

We knew the town was having an isolating effect on Melissa because of her inability to drive. We didn't want Chelmsford to become the next "resource room" for Melissa.

Identity

The pastor was standing in front of the altar reading off the names of each child to be baptized at an upcoming special mass. In the Catholic Church, it is customary to give your child a Christian name, preferably the name of a saint. The priest stopped when he came to Jason's name and looked at the assembled parents, babies, and godparents-to-be. He took a couple of steps forward down the center aisle and focused his gaze on us and the squirming six-month-old in my arms. Then, visibly annoyed, he said, "Jason Kim, what kind of name is that? I'll name him 'Marie' if I have to." Jack slid his hand along the pew and rested it on the side of my thigh. We both looked straight ahead at the priest—our passive facial expressions masking our extreme embarrassment. The priest stepped back and returned to his list. Jason's godfather was sitting next to me and without hardly moving his head, looked over at us with wide eyes of astonishment. Kim is a very common Korean surname, and it was part of Jason's official Korean name: Kim Hae Hoon. It was a small, documented piece of his heritage that we wanted him to have. This opinionated pastor could see that our squirming six-month-old was Asian. It didn't matter to him. As we were leaving the church, a younger priest, who had been standing in the back of the church and had witnessed the exchange, came up to us and offered to baptize Jason in a private ceremony. Jason's godfather later said, "It wasn't that the priest made that comment; it was that he was really going to do it."

When Jason was little, I had bought a children's book, which was a collection of Korean folk stories, to introduce Korean customs and history to both him and me, and to help him begin to explore his roots. He had absolutely no appetite for any of the stories and wasn't interested in anything Korean. But Jason did try to process who he was and how he got here. Most adoptees have their "adoption" story, and even though we told and retold the story of how he came to be adopted, we found he had created his own identity story: One day we were driving somewhere, and Melissa and Jason were in the back seat. Jason was about ten years old, doing his usual nonstop chatter. Melissa asked us something about the time she was in Korea, and Jason piped up, "I remember running along on the docks in Korea and eating pieces of raw fish that the fishermen threw to me."

"What!" Jack and I exclaimed. "Jason, you were only six months old when we adopted you." His statement was hilarious but also profound and sad. It was what he had envisioned in his mind to make sense of his being—his identity. It was his creation story. In his mind, he saw himself as having been a little boy, alone in the world, and determined to survive—the hero's tale.

Where had he come up with this story? Had there been anything that prompted its inception? Trying to get Jason to talk about it was impossible. He was on to the next subject or question as soon as Jack or I started talking about it. He never would elaborate on it, and I have often wondered if our initial burst of laughter destroyed his vivid, yet fragile narrative of himself.

One time, friends of ours who are Chinese, invited the four of us to a restaurant in Boston's Chinatown for Dim Sum. Their son and daughter were about the same age as Jason and were playmates. My friend, the children's mother, spoke Mandarin and did all the food ordering. Afterward, I asked Jason how he liked the restaurant. He was a picky eater, so I thought he was going to tell me how he didn't like such-and-such foods, but he answered, "I liked it because nobody looked like you or Dad—everybody looked like me!"

Melissa never focused on the issue of looking different. I truly believe it was due to being exposed to other burn victims when she was very young, and having friends who were in wheelchairs, had Down Syndrome, or otherwise looked "different." To Melissa, appearances didn't matter. But belonging and families did matter—a lot. One day, I picked her up at Middlesex Community College, MCC, where she was enrolled in a Transition Program that prepared students for the workplace. She jumped into the car and immediately blurted out, "Guess what? One of my teachers said she would help me find my family in Korea!" The sound of her voice told me she was very excited.

"Really? She wants to help you find your Korean family?" I said.

"Yes!"

"Hmmm."

Jack and I always believed Jason and Melissa deserved to know about their backgrounds, and now Melissa wanted to know about hers. I didn't take the conversation any further, and we listened to the radio for the rest of the ride home. But two thoughts kept circulating in my mind as I drove: Who was I to interfere in Melissa's search? And what would she do if she fully grasped that her family abandoned her, having apparently left her on the street?

Melissa knew she had been burned before she came to us, but I felt confident that was all she knew, remembered, or had processed. This search might make her face some hard facts. She was looking for her family. But was it a family? At home, holding my thoughts to one side, I talked with her, trying to determine what it was she was searching for. She has a difficult time expressing complex ideas and subjects, but that didn't mean she didn't have them.

"I want to go to Korea," she said.

"Why?"

"To see where it is."

"It would be wonderful to see Korea, but what do you think you'll find there?"

She didn't answer. Maybe it was too broad a question for her.

"Do you want to see where you were born?"

"Yeah."

"Anything else?" I asked.

"I don't know," she said. (This was a common refrain if she lost her train of thought or couldn't articulate something.)

"Do you want to find your birth mother and father?"

"Yes," she said, "and my brothers and sisters."

"Do you think they'll be happy to see you?"

"Yes!" she answered.

I could see she had a childlike, idealistic picture of her Korean family. "Your Korean family might not have brothers and sisters," I said. She thought about that and agreed that might be a possibility. I asked her to wait a little while on her instructor's offer, and she agreed. I knew that the possibility of Melissa's image of a happy, welcoming Korean family probably had a slim chance of being true, but…what if some part of her vision was real?

That night in our bedroom, I told Jack about Melissa's teacher's offer. We had always thought there was a possibility that Melissa was not fully Korean because every once in a while, when she stood in the sun, you could see a strand or two of dark auburn hair. Her hair was also coarse and thick, not the fine, silk-like hair Jason had. When Jason and Melissa had been adopted, Korean society had been very harsh on mixed-race children, and adoption was taboo since the child would not be of the same bloodline. Shame about having an illegitimate or mixed-race child led to many infant abandonments. But maybe Melissa hadn't been abandoned for those reasons. What if there had been a horrible accident and her family or mother couldn't care for her? What if the only option they had was to leave her? We didn't know if any of those scenarios were part of Melissa's story, but that awful image I had in my mind all those years ago, of a baby burned and suffering, returned with a sudden, painful fury.

I started to cry and then sob. Jack, the person who grounded me and understood me, took me in his arms as I soaked his shirtsleeve. When I was able to speak, I looked up at him through teary eyes and, with a trembling voice, cried, "This person knows nothing about Melissa's background. She has no idea of what Melissa went through to get to this place. What *we* went through." The sobbing began anew. "Who does she think she is…! And if she finds them? What would it do to Melissa if she was rejected again, if they didn't have any interest in her? How would I control myself if we ever met them? How could they leave her…to die?"

Jack let me cry it out, and, when I had settled down, suggested we help Melissa with her wish by contacting Connie Boll in Connecticut, who had found Melissa in the children's hospital/orphanage in Korea all those years earlier. Finding one's adoptive roots is an inevitable hunger that should be fed, but this simple, well-intentioned offer by a caring instructor had the potential to wreak havoc on our family, and I was having none of it.

We told Melissa about Dad's idea, and she agreed to our plan. Jack and I thought it would be next to impossible to find any family members (this was before the internet was widely used and Google searches were years away), so perhaps Connie would be the only link Melissa would ever have. I'm not exactly sure why, but the conversation with the instructor never came up again while she was at that school, and we didn't contact Connie Boll.

Relationships

Melissa loved adventure, but there wasn't enough excitement for her in town. Although she maintained contact with her Chelmsford friends, the weekends were getting lonely, and boys were becoming an important part of her circle. A friend from MCC mentioned that she was a member of Springboard and was having fun going to their activities. Springboard is a social club that provides social activities for teens and adults with learning differences. It is an arm of the organization Toward Independent Living and Learning (TILL), and all their activities are supervised by group leaders. Melissa signed up. Red Sox games, whitewater rafting, amusement parks, snowboarding, dances, harbor cruises; she did them all. But some required proper ID (a glass of wine on a harbor cruise, a beer at the Red Sox game, etc.). Melissa was twenty-one, and as much as we thought of her as a young girl, she needed an ID. The official card the DMV issued looked very similar to a driver's license, so her disappointment at not having her license quickly faded. She felt like the young adult she was becoming. She had a new group of friends and…a boyfriend.

She met Brian (not his real name) at a Springboard outing. He was always neatly dressed, usually in chino pants, loafers, and an Oxford or a polo shirt. You could tell his parents cared about his appearance and grooming, and that Brian had internalized that. Brian had a driver's license, but since he lived a distance from Chelmsford, he and Melissa would get together at Springboard events. Springboard handled transportation for its members by making sure all activities were accessible via public transportation. Distant trips involved a van or bus that would meet at a designated transportation terminal, accessible by bus or subway. Since we lived outside of the Greater Boston area, it meant we still had to drive her to either the destination or the transportation terminal. Brian's parents did the same "pick-up-drop-off" routine as well. We knew because we had met them one late, cold winter afternoon in Cambridge waiting for the snow-tubing trip bus to arrive. They were the only two people around, and they looked to be about our age, in their fifties.

We chatted and commented that it was great that Brian could get a driver's license and had his own car. His mother said, "Yes, but he hasn't a clue. We pay for the registration, insurance, and gas." She seemed exasperated. I could appreciate where she was coming from. The effort and sometimes money it takes to bring your disabled child through each milestone in life is enormous and endless. I could be very wrong, but that's the vibe I got from Brian's mom that afternoon. She sounded tired of all the work and money it took.

Melissa and Brian continued to date through Springboard outings, but occasionally, his parents would allow him to drive up to Chelmsford to see her. We found Brian rarely discussed issues or plans with his parents (at least that's what he told Melissa and us) and found it easier to call or talk to Jack when he got into jams. We would remind him he should speak to his parents, but Brian continued to ask for our help. Maybe for reasons we thought we understood, Jack and I felt Brian still needed more parenting. To us, he seemed somewhat immature and stubborn—even considering his learning disabilities.

One time, while driving up to Chelmsford in a heavy rainstorm, he pulled into the lane behind a large truck on the highway and panicked because the truck's tires were kicking up the water onto his windshield and he couldn't see clearly. He steered his car off the road and got stuck in the muddy grass beyond the shoulder pavement. He called Melissa upset and crying, and she told him to call his parents, but Brian wanted to talk to Jack. By the time Jack located him on the side of the highway, the state police had already arrived. Jack called a tow truck to get him out of the muddy grass, and eventually, with Jack following him in his car, Brian drove the rest of the way to our house.

Jack called Brian's father, while I sat at the kitchen table with Melissa and Brian. I asked Brian, "So what did the State Police do when they got to your car?" He said, "The policeman put his head in the car and told me to stop crying; the car was just stuck in the mud." It was hard not to smile, yet I felt for him. We used Brian's misadventure and near-miss as an example for Melissa to help her understand how driving could be dangerous. She was processing the difficulties and dangers of driving. Melissa always needed personalized, concrete examples of problems.

Our biggest challenge with Melissa and Brian was to oversee their plans without upsetting them. Somehow, together, the two of them were always planning events that needed to be talked over. Neither of them was good at predicting how long it would take to get somewhere and back, and how much something would cost. They did not appreciate our help. In their minds, they were over twenty-one and adults. They saw themselves as being able to navigate their lives with little oversight.

Over and over, Jack and I explained to Melissa that time, money, and planning were difficult things for her, and that she needed to ask for help with her plans. "Melissa, everybody has some kind of disability, or at least something they can't do," I'd often tell her. Melissa was also stubborn and would not ask for help until it was too late sometimes. Her immediate reaction to a discussion at this point would be tears of embarrassment, anger, defeat, and extreme frustration. She knew she could never understand numbers, time, dates, etc. She was so angry about it. Compounding this was the fact that she often couldn't explain the reasons behind her decisions and to be fair, many times they were valid. I was the person most often in the wrong during these discussions. I would get frustrated and be quick to jump to conclusions. It was Jack's patience with her over money issues that many times revealed these truths.

For instance, if we gave her more than enough money for a movie and snacks, I would want to know how she managed to spend all her money and get upset with her without letting her explain she had treated her friend to popcorn and a drink (which we all know costs more than a movie ticket). For most kids, it would be easy to just say, "But I bought my friend some popcorn and a soda!" However, if she sensed anger, Melissa would go quiet, which made it difficult to get to an explanation. Many a time we blamed her for something, and it would be hours or days before we could put all the pieces of the story together.

An Angel on the Train

The importance of having a job, initially, had little meaning for Melissa. Jack helped her get her first job working as an office assistant, but, due to downsizing, it was eliminated after a year and a half. I picked her up on her last day of work and had rolled down the car window to enjoy the warm summer breeze while I tried to think of things to say to cheer her up, since I was expecting tears. Instead, Melissa was beaming as she walked across the parking lot. Her long black hair accentuated the pretty floral dress she was wearing. She was carrying a gift bag and a large balloon. "They had a party for me! And a cake!" she exclaimed. She pulled out a small gift, along with a card signed by everyone, and a letter of recommendation from her supervisor. To her, it might as well have been the last day of school before summer vacation.

A vocational counselor at MA Rehab began exploring work options with her. For her first interview, Melissa was eager to answer questions about potential jobs. She was smiling and sitting forward in her chair, opposite the counselor who sat behind a desk.

"So, what do you like to do, Melissa? What are you good at?"

"I like people," Melissa said. "I want to be around people."

"And what do you find difficult to do, Melissa?"

Melissa's smile disappeared. She had undergone comprehensive testing every three years since she was in preschool, and now here was another person evaluating her abilities. Her lip trembled, and she said, "I can't do math, and sometimes reading is hard." Then the tears fell. The counselor handed her a tissue and said, "Don't worry, we'll find a job for you." That seemed to cheer her up. Melissa could be sad, but with the right comment, she would be happy and smiling again a moment later.

Most of the jobs she applied for through Mass Rehab had an element of the job that she couldn't perform or could do only with the help of a job coach, which they told her they could provide. However, the job search did not get her discouraged. You could say she was resilient, but closer to the truth was the fact that Melissa loved to meet people, and job interviews were just another opportunity to see and talk to someone. While there were numerous interviews, nineteen months went by with no results. Her counselor suggested she should volunteer at Action for Boston Community Development (ABCD), a nonprofit human services organization in Boston. We all jumped at it. We had already decided that Melissa needed to live in a city that had public transportation, and a job in Boston would be an excellent beginning to making city living a reality.

She had no qualms about taking the train to Boston and quite enjoyed it. Ever the socializer, it didn't take her long to find a group of fellow commuters.

"So, how's the train working out, Melissa?" Jack asked.

"Good. I sit with some friends every morning."

She explained that two of the commuters were married and the other two were just friends.

"Do you sit in the same seats?" I asked.

"Yeah."

"How do the five of you all sit together?"

"We sit in the seats that face each other."

"Oh, and are they older than you?"

"Yeah."

It was an eclectic group to be sure, but that didn't faze Melissa. She looked forward to her commute each day, settling into a nice routine. Arriving at the station in Boston, she'd walk about a quarter of a mile to the North End (the Italian section) where she worked with a group of grandmotherly older women who told her where to get the best lunches. Melissa could never fully explain to us what she did there beyond answering the phone, but it was a positive experience for her. After ten months of volunteering, ABCD told Melissa they did not have any openings available for her. Now it was twenty-nine months—almost two and a half years—still no job. Melissa continued to volunteer while resuming her job search, and Jack and I were wondering if she would ever get a job.

Then "Clarence," or Larry, came to her rescue. To explain, Larry was a member of the commuter train buddies. We called him "Clarence" because he gave Melissa her Christmas present: what she had been trying to get for over two years—a job. (We were thinking of Clarence in Frank Capra's classic Christmas movie *It's a Wonderful Life.*) One night in December, Melissa came home from work and said she thought she might have a job.

We thought she was talking about ABCD or maybe a lead that the Jewish Vocational Services (JVS) had passed on to her. (JVS was another agency that worked with Mass Rehab.) However, it turned out that Larry liked Melissa's perky personality and knew she had been looking for a job for quite a long time. Melissa said, "He told me to sharpen my pencil!" The next week, Larry offered her a job at the law firm where he worked.

While we were happy Melissa might get a job, we soon became concerned. Larry wanted Melissa to come into the office on a Sunday afternoon so he could show her what he wanted her to do on the Monday morning. Okay, now we wanted to meet this guy. We were not going to let her go to any office with some man on a Sunday afternoon. We told Melissa we would drive her into Boston, and we wanted to meet Larry before she went anywhere.

On Sunday, we drove to an older office building located a block from the downtown shopping area and pulled up to the curb outside of the building's glass entrance doors and waited for Larry to come down. Melissa met him in the lobby. He was impeccably dressed in a suit and tie. He was a charming, congenial, and well-mannered gentleman…who was in his seventies. It surprised Larry that Melissa hadn't mentioned his age (age, numbers, math again…it didn't matter to Melissa). We had a good laugh. He was mortified when he realized our concern. It hadn't occurred to him we would see him as a threat.

He was our "Christmas Angel." He even had a striking resemblance to Clarence in the movie. His mouth and eyes were very similar. Larry was also about the same height; five-foot-five with shoes on, had a thinning hairline—albeit a little trimmer around the waist than Clarence, and the same warm, generous smile. He had old-school manners and always wore a suit and tie when he went out in public. As if he had walked out of a 1940s movie.

Larry wanted Melissa to help him organize his office. He was an accountant (what?) at a nonprofit poverty and law policy center and needed someone to help straighten up his papers. It dumbfounded us. Larry was about to learn how Melissa handled organizing, sorting, and picking things up. Those skills were almost as bad as her math. Melissa came home that first day and said, "Mom, Dad, there are paper files up to the ceiling!"

"In Larry's office?" we asked.

"Yes, and in the boss's office too!"

I wasn't sure just how much help Melissa provided with straightening up, but Larry had noticed that computers did not intimidate her. A computer was not his de facto office tool that winter of 2003 and when the company updated the accounting software that Larry was using, he wanted Melissa to use it. Around the same time Melissa started working, Larry realized he also needed one-on-one help with the new software, so Jonas was hired. Besides assisting Larry, Jonas oversaw Melissa's computer duties. He looked out for her, breaking down tasks and double-checking her daily entries. Every week we half expected Melissa to come home and say the job wasn't working out. Just the opposite happened. They were sending Jonas and Melissa to a training session to learn how to use the new software. Was this a joke? Was this some way to make her fail so they could fire her? It wasn't a joke, and they didn't want to fire her. They recognized a skill she had. If only her fourth-grade teacher could see this, I thought.

When Melissa was in fourth grade, we had an IBM PC Junior that we all used for its word processor function. It was exceedingly primitive, but Melissa took to it immediately. Handwriting was difficult and taxing for her, and when homework required her to write answers to questions, it added time and tears. Being able to press a letter on the keyboard and create a legible letter on the page was almost miraculous to her. Computers were new tools at that time, and her teachers had not wanted her to use it for homework. "How do I know if you aren't doing her homework for her?" one teacher had said to me, at the time. I was insulted. "Why would I do that? This is new technology that Melissa can use, and I think it will help a lot."

Melissa was understanding the value of her job, and being selected to attend a seminar gave her a feeling of importance and a sense of pride in her work. Larry knew he would retire soon, and I always felt he had hired Melissa to keep him company and help her fill in her resume for the next job.

Years later, I invited Jonas to lunch with Melissa and me, and Jonas told me, "No matter how the day was going, or how I was feeling, I knew if I went into Larry's office, Melissa and Larry would always have a smile for me. They made my day brighter." I asked him about the "files up to the ceiling." "All true," he said.

Resignations

Melissa needed to live in a city that had public transportation. But what would a move to the city do to the family compound in Chelmsford? Both of my parents had passed away, and the soul of the place had changed. Still, it came as a tremendous surprise when my niece, Erin, announced that she, her husband, and her daughter Alexis, were moving to Florida and my sister and her husband were going with them—the whole gang. We had thought we would be the first to move and had been harboring a sense of guilt about leaving them. Guilt turned into sadness as I watched a new family move into my parents' house. Their property line ended at the gate leading to the old stone fireplace outside our bedroom window. No longer could I walk through that gate or pick the pink roses that grew on the arbor—the ones that always bloomed around my birthday—or walk by the small stone pool under the fir trees that dropped the small cones that Jason had been so afraid to step on with bare feet when he was little. Nor could I pass the ever-spreading blueberry bush where Matthew and Erin had competed with the birds for juicy berries every June. The path between the houses no longer existed. The umbilical cord was severed. But with the cutting of an umbilical cord, a new life begins; a new set of genes is passed to the next generation. Reflecting on this and the loss of my beloved compound brought to mind my most vivid memory of Dad and Luther:

Dad and I were standing in the upper field under an apple tree. Luther and Dad must have had some previous conversation about the trees, because, as Luther approached, he took the pipe out of his mouth and nodded toward the tree. "Thought you might want to know how to graft those trees." "Sure," Dad said. Without saying anything more, Luther pulled out a sharp pocketknife, reached up, cut off a thin apple branch, and whittled the end into a V-shape. We followed him to a different variety of tree and he cut a similar-sized branch and held it in front of Dad. "Cut this end like a slit then notch the two branches together." Pointing with the tip of his knife, he said, "Make sure the green layers, just under the bark of the two branches, are lined up. See right there?" I nudged my father so I could see as he inserted the pointed V-shaped branch into the groove. He then told Dad how to wind twine around the two branches and coat it with bee's wax. Luther was showing Dad how to get an apple tree shoot of one variety to produce the fruit of the grafted section. He was giving Dad a botany lesson, and I was mesmerized.

When Dad was still working, he'd often remark that he wished he could putter around the yard all day like Luther. There was an open field between his gardens and our property, so it wasn't unusual to see Luther and his dog walking the rows of vegetable plants, or pruning and spraying fruit trees, or doing whatever the day demanded.

Luther was the link to our property's past. He knew its history. He told Dad and me about the old Perham cider mill just outside the town center, where the apples from our orchard were brought. I even remember riding my bike past that old cider mill before it was razed to make way for the new interstate 495.

If only I could go back in time and ask Luther to tell his stories…
If only I could ask him about my pear-apple tree…

But now the compound was no more. My acute sense of loss made me determined to keep the memory of all the things I loved about that property alive. I refused to let it fade.

We eventually sold our home, moved to Boston, and set Melissa up in a small studio apartment across the street from us. Independent living—that germ of an idea we had when she was in nursery school was becoming a reality. It became our focus.

Melissa and Brian had been dating for seven years. She was thirty-one and Brian was about twenty-eight. While still needing some guidance, they felt entitled to all the benefits of adulthood; however, they had a very naïve outlook on just how adulthood worked. It was easy to talk to them when they first started dating because they were with their Springboard group and were chaperoned, but as the years went on, it became more difficult. Boyfriends, sex, relationships, money: as delicate and challenging as it was to talk to Melissa about these subjects, we felt somebody needed to be talking to Brian about them too, but that was not our role. Melissa was caught between her boyfriend and us many times. After some of our talks, we would ask Melissa if Brian had discussed anything with his parents. "No," or "I don't know," were her usual answers. Brian had a job, got a paycheck, had a car, and, in his judgment, was an adult who by this stage didn't appreciate another set of parents.

"Brian, you really need to talk to your parents about these things, especially about getting married," Jack said.

"No, I don't."

The issues had come to a head. Brian was talking about getting married and having children. His idea of marriage and children was as simplistic as Melissa's idea of finding her perfect Korean family.

"Brian, have you talked to your parents about this?" Jack asked.

"I told my mother I wanted to give Melissa an engagement ring."

"Did you talk to your parents about getting married?"

He was silent. "This is big, Brian," I said. "You need to talk to them. There are lots of things to think about."

Jack and I sort of knew where this was going and wanted Brian to slow down. So, once again, we tried to talk through the issues with them. Brian was still living at home and had no experience living on his own. We suggested he talk to his parents about that option first, to see if that might be a possibility. It didn't go over too well. Weeks and weeks went by, and I finally asked Melissa, "Did Brian ever talk to his mother about getting an apartment?"

"I don't know," she replied. It was clearly a subject Brian didn't want to talk about with anyone, not even Melissa.

Transportation was another issue that entered the discussion. Brian lived about twenty miles from Boston and drove to the commuter station to take the train into the city where he had a job. (Brian told us his mother didn't want him to drive into the city.) I knew living that distance from the city would affect Melissa's independence, but I didn't know if Melissa understood the problem. Oh, but she did.

"How do you feel about living in—"

"I'm not moving," she said.

"Why?"

"Because…because I won't be able to use the T (public transportation) and I won't be able to see my friends or go to work!"

Brian didn't take any steps to move out of his parents' home, and Melissa was adamant that she wasn't moving out of the city. Perhaps it was from Melissa's experiences living by herself for the past two years, but it seemed to us she was more mature than Brian. But the BIG discussion was, of course, children.

One evening, Brian and Melissa were sitting at our kitchen counter happily telling us about having children. Jack and I were standing opposite them on the other side of the counter. Without coming right out and saying it would be beyond their capabilities at that time to raise a child, we tried to get them to understand what raising a child would involve, and that maybe it wasn't such a simple idea. It was the first of many, many conversations we had trying to get them to understand the issues. We gave them concrete examples of what everyday life might look like by giving them "what if" baby scenarios. We knew their salaries barely gave them any extra spending money, even with both sets of parents subsidizing their living expenses, so Jack began by asking, "How are you going to be able to afford to buy baby clothes or baby food?"

"What are you going to do if the baby is sick at night?" I chimed in.

They didn't answer. I could see Melissa's eyes watering up

and Brian bristling. The discussion ended for the time being. But every time they brought the subject up, we'd raise another scenario with them. "Where would your child go to school?" "How would you get to the school?" "What if your child wanted to play sports, and you couldn't afford to pay for the sports gear?" "How would you tell your child 'no'?" Unfortunately, each scenario we laid out only made Brian angrier and more resolute in his desire to have children.

Melissa was perturbed and upset. Brian wasn't budging on his decisions about their future, and Jack and I were not giving up on trying to explain to them. One day they came over and Brian announced he still wanted to get married. This time Jack was blunt and told them pointedly what they didn't want to hear. "Look, guys, we're not against you two having a relationship, but marriage and especially children are not good ideas right now, and neither one of you can handle money well." We were sitting on the sofa and Brian was standing across the room next to Melissa. He glared at us in silence, with his arms by his sides, hands curled in semi-fists, and his body posture betraying his anger. Then he said, "Well, I want to have children." He turned around and said, "I'm going home," and walked out.

    He left Melissa behind. We knew the thing that bothered her the most about her life was her inability to understand math. It complicated everything. Jack put his arm around her, lowered his voice, and as gently as he could, said, "Melissa, imagine your baby is now in first grade. How would you know how much lunch money to give him? Then he comes home with math homework. How would you be able to help him with that? What would you do?"

She didn't answer. She looked up and stared beyond us. She was processing it. She was beginning to understand the difficulties. Then she looked at us and with an edge in her voice said, "I get it." Melissa later admitted it had scared her. From that moment on, she knew having a baby would be frightening and impossible for her to manage. We weren't so successful with Brian. He was beyond upset. He was angry with us, and he thought we didn't like him. I have to admit, his stubbornness tested our patience, and we got angry and had heated conversations more than once throughout this period.

That fall, while at an outing with some of their Springboard friends, Brian gave Melissa an engagement ring. In his mind, they were getting married. Obstacles be damned! Melissa wasn't so sure. She took his ring, but she told me afterward, "Mom, I was mad. He did it in front of everyone! He still wants a baby." She was having second thoughts. She couldn't convince him a baby would be a mistake. Besides, she knew how difficult living on your own could be. Keeping her apartment clean and organized was not her best strength, and somehow, no matter how hard she tried, she could not resist the temptation to withdraw "magic money" from the ATM at the neighborhood bank down the street.

Fate intervened that following summer when she introduced Brian to a girl she knew from MCC. Brian decided he was more interested in the new friend. Melissa was hurt and furious. Reflecting on her problems with Brian, Melissa, quite unexpectedly, informed us she had talked to her nurse practitioner and had scheduled a tubal ligation. It was a sudden and startling announcement, but we knew from past experiences with both Jason and Melissa, advice that was initially rejected was sometimes heeded eventually. Melissa was determined to have control over her life. Oh, and the ring? She put it in a simple envelope and mailed it to Brian's home.

Fighting Back

When Larry retired from the Law Reform Institute, it had been understood that Melissa's position would be eliminated, and she would have to look for another job. Surprisingly, the company had asked her to stay on board for a couple more months to help with the accounting software transition, which had boosted her pride immensely. After that, the job search began anew. Nine months had passed, and after numerous job interviews for positions that had not been compatible with her abilities, Jewish Vocational Services (JVS) finally found an appropriate job for Melissa as a support clerk in the Department of Veterans Affairs in downtown Boston.

Helping her fill out all the new-hire paperwork, it amazed us to see all the benefits and job security a government job could give you. According to the forms she signed, Melissa had a one-year probationary period, and after that time, if her work was satisfactory, she would be entitled to all government benefits. She was confident she could handle the work, and her past work experiences proved she was conscientious and dependable.

Melissa found the job stressful at times because she had to focus on making sure she didn't transpose any numbers or letters on the files, but overall, she was happy and proud of her work. She got an excellent six-month job review and even got a letter of recognition from her supervisor.

Then she got a new boss.

Two days away from the one-year probation period end-date, when she would get full benefits, she came over to have dinner with us. She walked in and stood next to me. I had just bent down to pick something off the floor when Melissa blurted out, "I was fired." I didn't look up. I fixated on her feet for a moment, trying to handle the rush of emotions. Standing up, I saw Melissa's lips trembling, and tears rolling down her cheeks.

"What happened?" I said.

"I don't know," she sobbed.

"Were you late for work?"

"No, never," she angrily replied.

"Did you do something wrong?"

"No!" she yelled.

How could this have happened? What about that great job performance review she had got from her last supervisor only a couple of months ago? Her new supervisor reported to her counselor at JVS in October, only two months earlier, that she was "doing well." Melissa continued to cry, and we couldn't get an explanation out of her as to why she was fired. What had she done? She must have done something, or not done something. What was it? We were upset with Melissa at first, peppering her with questions. It took a while, but eventually, she was able to explain that while her old boss would break down the job tasks, and explain exactly what she wanted, her new boss never did that, and worse, never listened to her when she told him she needed help. Melissa was not afraid to speak up and had made it known to him on numerous occasions that she could get a job coach to help her break down the tasks. She knew that having a job coach was a service that individuals with disabilities are entitled to under the Americans with Disabilities Act. Job coaches don't do the work but can help break down complicated tasks or organize work for the individual, much like Jonas had done at her previous job, but her new boss had kept telling her it wasn't necessary. "We'll work on it," he told her, but Melissa said he had never actually offered to help her.

She wasn't given a warning, much less anything in writing. Just terminated. Anyone in the "circle of disabilities" knows that a job really depends on a supervisor's acceptance of the disability. Even if you can perform the job tasks (one must be able to do the essential parts of the job), if the supervisor doesn't accept you, your position is at risk, and it's only a matter of time before you could be fired. It's a hard, cold fact.

Around the time of our Disability Awareness Week, I had taken a course to educate myself about Chapter 766, the MA Special Education law, and to become a parent-advocate to help other parents navigate the system and better advocate for their child at IEP meetings. The instructor was Robert K. Crabtree, the attorney who co-drafted Chap 766 (the first Special Education law, which became the model for the first federal special education law in 1975). But after working with a second family in a second neighboring school system, I quickly realized that no matter what rights parents or students had under the law, school administrators could interpret or ignore those laws according to their views. These parents were asking for accommodations that were readily given to children in our town. The only way they could get fair treatment was either to continually fight the system or threaten legal action. Neither of which they wanted to consider as options. I could only arm them with a knowledge of the law. I wasn't enough of a pit bull to be an effective advocate; frankly, I had stunk at it. That experience had ended my advocating attempt, but I had learned how to fight back for Melissa, if ever needed, and this was the time.

Did Melissa make mistakes at this job? Probably, but her termination was unfair. No warning of poor job performance, coupled with a previous great job review, a new supervisor, and being fired two days before permanent benefits would begin, raised red flags for Jack and me. Jack called the Disability Law Center, Inc. in Boston and spoke to the senior lawyer. After explaining Melissa's situation, the lawyer wasn't sure if they could take the case because of their caseload but would review it with the other lawyers in the office and would get back to us. Jack was worried. Uncertainty: It was a condition that lingered in the gut of our stomachs. So many of Melissa's needs were in the hands of others. It's easy to fight for yourself. It's downright emotional to fight for your child.

The Law Center accepted her case, and they filed a complaint of job discrimination and failure to accommodate against the Department of Veterans Affairs. The mediation session was held in a conference room in the Government Building with Melissa's supervisor, his HR manager, Jack, Melissa, and me, and the lawyers and a mediator in attendance. Melissa's supervisor sat at one end of the conference table and the mediator sat at the other end. Melissa sat between Jack and me, and the disability law lawyer sat next to Jack. On the other side of the table was the supervisor's human resource manager and their lawyer. Melissa's supervisor began by stating that Melissa was not doing tasks correctly; she was leaving files on counters, and a file was missing, so Melissa must have shredded it. Our lawyer then put simple, straightforward questions to him:

"Was Melissa ever given prior notice of a poor job performance?"

"No."

"Do you have any documentation of reasons for termination?"

"No."

"Do you have a copy of her recent positive job review?"

"No."

"Did you ever provide any job assistance?"

"No."

"Melissa, do you have anything you want to say?" the mediator asked.

I thought she might become weepy, but she sat up straight in her chair, looked at her lawyer, and in a voice tinged with anger said, "I told him I needed help, and I said I needed a job coach, but he didn't help me."

At that point, they asked us to wait outside while the lawyers and mediator discussed the case. Our lawyer returned after a few minutes and said Melissa had proven her case. Due to the lack of any documentation on the Veterans Department's side, they would have to give Melissa her job back, she could have a job coach, and they would expunge any record of her termination in her personnel file. The bad news was she would have the same boss, and they would extend her probationary period for another year. We had to accept the mediator's decision, but how does somebody manage to stay in a job for a year when your boss clearly has a target on your back? The supervisor would undoubtedly keep documentation now.

JVS provided a job coach for Melissa, but we knew she could not insulate her against further repercussions. After a couple of weeks, the four of us met, and Melissa's job coach said Melissa was absolutely being targeted and it looked like they were going to "job performance" her out of the job, only this time they would have documentation. She said, "Melissa's doing a good job, but she's being criticized for doing the same things other employees are doing, and sometimes her boss criticizes her for things she didn't do. He's out to find any little thing he can fault her for."

Melissa was very unhappy, and her coach thought it would be a good idea if she quit before they could fire her again. We all agreed. Melissa quit on her terms. She didn't give them the opportunity to terminate her. The job wasn't worth the stress or discrimination. It didn't matter how long the next job search would be.

Melissa's biggest strength was her personality. She loved to meet people. She always had a smile for you. We thought about this one night while we were at our favorite cinema in Cambridge. Why couldn't Melissa be a ticket-taker? She'd love greeting moviegoers. We brought home an application, and after Melissa explained in her interview that she wouldn't be able to help behind the counter with customers if it involved money, she got the part-time job.

Getting to the job involved a commute, which made time

management critical: Melissa took a bus (the bus stop was near her condo building) to Boston's "Downtown Crossing" stop. From there she walked a block to the subway station and took a train across the river to Cambridge's Kendall Square. After she exited the subway, it was about a quarter-of-a-mile walk to the theater. Missing the bus or subway train meant waiting for the next one, and that meant being late for work. And the ever-present and not-uncommon delays buses and subways experienced also meant being late for work. To handle the problem without making it complicated, Melissa left an hour earlier than necessary. The commute home was always easier—we picked her up. Taking the subway was not a safe option at midnight. Jack and I didn't mind the drive at all. We both love to take rides through the city at night. I think cities morph into whole different magical places when the lights come on. My favorite moments were driving home across the beautiful Longfellow Bridge with the city skyline ahead and a full moon shining on the silent sailboats moored on the Charles River. Even without the full moon, it was a view we looked forward to every time we picked her up.

Melissa loved working, and except for bitter, cold, rainy, or snowy days, the commute didn't bother her. In fact, she was proud that she could navigate both Boston and Cambridge by herself via public transportation. She was older now and appreciated our concerns back in Chelmsford about driving: she admitted that having a car in the city would have been more than she could handle or afford.

After our experience with the government job, we asked Melissa to introduce us to her supervisor, which she did one night. Howie seemed like a good guy, and Jack asked him to give us a heads-up if there was a problem with Melissa's work or if anything wasn't working out. He agreed. We'd run into him after a movie occasionally, but otherwise, all was well: no problems. One night, when we picked Melissa up after work, she got in the car and said, "Guess who I saw?" It was a familiar refrain because she liked to tell us if she saw any of our friends. But before we could play the guessing game, she blurted out, "John Keller!"

It took a minute for us to figure out who she was talking about.

"Did you say 'Hi?'" I asked.

"Yeah, I took his ticket and said, 'Hi, Mr. Keller.'"

"Was he surprised?" Jack asked.

"Very," said Melissa with a laugh.

It was especially funny to Jack and me because John Keller was a political commentator on the local news and wasn't a regular news anchorperson. After we dropped Melissa off at her apartment, I turned to Jack and said, "Melissa watches the news?"

Edge of Darkness

Women with disabilities have a 40 percent greater chance of becoming a victim of domestic and sexual abuse than their peers. One of Melissa's resource teachers took me aside when Melissa was a senior in high school and warned me about that possibility. She didn't put it in any statistical or numerical way: she just wanted me to understand the darker side of the world and how vulnerable Melissa might be. I think she sensed I was naïve about the danger. She was right. We focused almost exclusively on Melissa's daily living skills. Surely, we could keep an eye on her boyfriends, we thought… and then *he* swept in…and it almost killed us.

After their second date, he told her, "I'm moving in with you. My lease is up, and I don't have any place to live." Melissa took out her phone and said, "I have to ask my parents if that's okay." He took the phone away from her and said, "Don't tell your parents."

"They're gonna find out!" she said.

"Let them," he replied.

Within a matter of two weeks, he had moved into her apartment, isolated her, convinced her we didn't love her, and taken control before anyone realized what was happening. Melissa had dinner with us most nights, and when we asked her simple questions about how her day had gone, she'd just go silent on us. She was being evasive. Something was wrong. Weeks went by. We weren't sure what the problem was, so we invited her and her new "boyfriend" over to talk with us. Randy followed Melissa into our apartment, carrying himself confidently with his chin slightly raised while looking around our unit like he was appraising it. A little odd and arrogant for someone who knew what we were about to find out. We invited them to sit down on a small sofa in the living room; over the next two hours, everything he told us was disturbing, and, yes, he had moved in with Melissa.

Jack and I both distinctly remember him pausing, leaning back slightly, and reaching over for Melissa's hand. He put his hand on top of hers, and with a smile that revealed his upper front teeth, he looked at us—not Melissa—and ever so calmly said, "We love each other." I wanted to vomit. Jack shifted sideways in his chair, put his arm over the back of it, and rested his hand on the side of his forehead. He was trying to control his anger. We were in a serious psychological tug-of-war for Melissa…and this guy had the advantage.

We kept talking, hoping maybe they could see this wasn't the best living arrangement. We told him we would give him two weeks to find another apartment. There was something about this guy that just wasn't right. Jack and I knew it and knew that we had to get him out of Melissa's apartment. My mind was racing. I was trying to understand him. I was struck by his movements, or, more accurately, lack of them. He was sitting back on the sofa with a relaxed look on his face. Jack and I were doing all the talking. He seemed contentedly passive. He wasn't trying to convince us he had no place to live. He wasn't trying to convince us of anything. And then, with all the assurance that day would be followed by night, he sighed, and said, "Melissa and I are eventually going to move away." It was what we feared the most! Melissa was over twenty-one. If she agreed to go away with him, we had no legal rights to prevent it.

Feeling the pulse of my heart pounding in my ears, I calmly said to him, "Do you know that Melissa has disabilities, and a lot of her services are in the city? Her job is in Cambridge, and she needs to live in a city with public transportation." He didn't react to any of it, and tellingly, I had noticed that after he put his hand on Melissa's and proclaimed their love, he removed it and never looked at her again or included her in the conversation. She was inconsequential. Melissa smiled weakly when he proclaimed their "love," but otherwise, she was detached from the conversation. But the big problem was Melissa. We already sensed a new resentment from her and didn't want to alienate her to the point she would run off with him, especially after Brian. We were afraid Melissa had partly blamed us for their breakup—we thought she might believe that we didn't want her to have a serious boyfriend.

After that day, it became harder and harder for us to see her. Randy made it clear to her that we were not to pick her up after work anymore. Yet, he refused to pick her up and made her take the subway home—at midnight. We felt we had to somehow make him understand we weren't trying to keep Melissa all to ourselves, so we invited him to join our family for Thanksgiving at Jason's home where he could meet everyone, including Matthew, who was coming up from NYC. Jason had become the homebody of the family, and having everyone together to celebrate the holidays was important to him (even though he was probably going to announce to friends and family alike, that at nine o'clock he was going to bed).

At Jason's, Randy displayed a polite demeanor, choosing mostly to sit quietly, adding little to the general hubbub of conversations. He didn't exhibit any of the troubling behaviors we had witnessed in Boston, and for one fleeting afternoon, both Jack and I hoped the worst had passed. Melissa was her old self; happy to see everyone, especially her niece and nephew—Jason's children. Jack and I didn't want to focus on Randy. We just wanted to enjoy our boys and our grandchildren. Jack said later, the thought in the back of his head was: Can I live with this? My thoughts were darker. I was hoping the visit would convince Randy that our family could embrace him if he wanted to reach out, but I was afraid it was all an act. Jason and Matthew thought he was quiet—otherwise, they thought he seemed just fine.

Weeks went by and Randy was still living at Melissa's, so trying to deal with the situation a little differently, we invited them over for brunch. Jack wanted to get him alone and suggested they walk to the bakery for pastries. He wanted to know what plans he had for moving out, because all we ever got from Melissa was, "I don't know." Jack asked him if he had found an apartment, and he calmly replied, "Well, to be honest, Mr. Tumminello, I haven't been looking." Not wanting to have an argument on the street, Jack curtly told him, "Well, you need to find one fast and you need to move out." Describing the conversation to me that afternoon, Jack said, "Did he think the 'well, to be honest, Mr. Tumminello' nonsense would disarm me? He has no intention of moving out."

I thought about turning to friends for support, but Melissa's situation wasn't an easy conversation I could have with them. I remember walking to a restaurant with friends who had come into town for dinner. I began talking about some issues we were dealing with, but realized I had to stop my prattling. We were grieving, and there was no way I could explain what we were going through. And some friends didn't seem to grasp our angst. What could we say? He had succeeded in isolating Melissa from all her friends and her brothers. We could see that he was convincing Melissa that she was worthless and only he could love her. It was insidious and evil. The only thing left now was for him to separate Jack and me from her. He was dangerous and we were in the fight of our lives for Melissa.

The situation was taking a toll on Jack and me. Every night after dinner we spent hours trying to come up with a plan to make the nightmare go away, and every time poor Matthew called, we assaulted him with our worries. What were we going to do? What could we do? Jack and I thought about those two questions every waking moment of every day. Our boys still thought we were being too hard on the guy, but they weren't around to witness any of the exchanges and see the difference in Melissa's attitude toward us. Matthew still didn't appear concerned. He told us, "Mom, Dad, you kinda *do* treat her like a teenager; you need to let her live her life." He didn't see the problem as we saw it and still held the opinion that we were being too hard on the guy and trying to micro-manage Melissa's life. Jason agreed. That was a deep, deep hurt. They saw the issue solely as being about Melissa being able to have a live-in boyfriend. Couples Melissa's age did that all the time, they told us. We knew that, and I suppose if she were still dating Brian, and the baby issue had been resolved, we would have been okay with that—they would have been cramped for space, but otherwise fine. But not this guy. He didn't resemble a boyfriend. Matthew and Jason didn't understand what Melissa's day-to-day difficulties entailed and how easily her life could be destroyed.

Randy was isolating her more and more each day, and it was a feat that she even kept her job at the cinema. When we did get to talk to Melissa, she was angry with us, and there was a new level of meanness in her conversations. In all her thirty-three years, I couldn't remember Melissa being that mean. She had spent her life wanting to be accepted and loved by everyone. Meanness was not in her emotional makeup. This wasn't Melissa.

We had seen Melissa just a couple of times since Thanksgiving, so when Randy invited Jack and me to his mother's Christmas party, we agreed to go. The only way to enter the small house on the night of the party was via the back door, which led directly into a cramped kitchen that was crowded with people and food. Although there were only about ten or twelve people in the kitchen, because of the size of the room, everyone was squeezed around the counters eating or sitting at the kitchen table, which was in the center of the room. Randy and Melissa were wedged between guests and sitting at the table facing us as we entered. Melissa saw us, smiled, and said, "Hi." Randy looked up, made eye contact with us, and kept eating. It was as if he was telegraphing to us, *You're in my backyard now.* With hardly any space to move or stand, and not recognizing anybody, we moved into the only other room available, where a small Christmas tree was set up. There we found a few other guests. It seemed that family members were the ones in the kitchen. No one mingled during the party. Balancing paper plates of food on our laps, we whispered to each other that the party seemed odd.

As the party was winding down, Randy and Melissa came into the room and sat on the couch opposite us. Randy's mother appeared and remarked how happy they looked. Jack and I said nothing. I felt a strange disassociation watching Melissa. It was like a wave of extreme homesickness—that feeling of strangeness and of wanting to go home so badly that it hurts to breathe. I wanted to rewind the last three months, like they never happened—make them disappear. I wanted to grab Melissa, pull her over, and sit her down between Jack and me. I wanted to see Jack put his arm around her. I wanted her to look up and smile at him like she did in so many family pictures. I wanted to snuggle up against her arm, entwine my arm around hers, and squeeze her hand and never let go. I wanted our daughter back.

Randy announced that he and Melissa were leaving, and it wasn't long after that, that the party broke up. I said a quick goodbye to Randy's mother and practically bolted out the door. I didn't look back or wait for Jack. My emotions and fears were too big for those tiny, cramped rooms in that tiny, small house. I was suffocating. The sharp, frigid air stung my face and burned my lungs, yet I welcomed it with each deep breath. The sky was dark and expansive, and I welcomed that too. I wanted my torment to fade into the shadows of night and lift up to the skies—unseen, diaphanous, and appeased. I got in the cold car still watching the sky and wishing to escape reality. It was only a minute or two before I heard the car door open. Jack got in the driver's seat and sat still for a moment. I wasn't paying attention to him, but then he broke the silence. He turned to me and said, "I can't believe what Randy's mother just said to me."

"What?" I asked, coming out of my night-dream.

"She said, 'Thanks for coming, you should know…he'll never hurt her.'"

Still stunned, Jack said, "Who says that? That's not normal!"

Unreachable You

Jack and I hosted our family Christmas that year, and Melissa made it across the street to join us. But she didn't come over the next day to see Matthew. The day after Christmas was a big deal for Melissa, Jack, and me. It meant we got to spend a little more time with Matthew since we saw him so infrequently. He lived and had his own business in New York City, and we all missed him. Matthew called her several times that day and left a message that he was leaving for New York, and wanted to say goodbye, but she never came over. She never called him back—the brother she adored. Before Matthew left, the three of us went out for a late lunch. We were walking on the sidewalk outside our building, when we spotted Melissa across the street leaving a convenience store with a bag in her hand. She looked rushed and worried. A trip to the store was usually an event for Melissa. It was a chance to say hello. It was "city entertainment" and always left her smiling. We all started yelling, "Melissa! Melissa!" to get her attention. She had her head down and just kept hurrying along toward her condo building. "It's cold out and she has her hat on. Maybe she can't hear us," Matthew said. Jack and I looked at each other. We knew. We recognized each other's anguish—Melissa was so close, and yet unreachable.

A month before Melissa had met Randy, she had signed up for a midwinter week-long cruise to Mexico with a group from Springboard. Jack and I had helped her plan out what she needed to do before the trip. Melissa had made arrangements to take time off from work, had gotten her passport, and had saved up for months for the trip. We had helped with the extra money she needed, plus some fun money to spend on herself. She was excited about it. As the cruise date neared, I helped Melissa with her outfits, but that was squeezed into the time Randy was at work and was mostly done over the phone. I managed to get her out one afternoon to shop for her trip and have lunch—the one time I was able to go out with her. Randy called her from work, and when he found out what we were doing, he called her every couple of minutes—incessantly. I wanted to yell, "Hang up on the bastard!" Instead, I asked her if she could shut her phone off. But Melissa got angry and refused. That's when I knew for sure, that if Jack and I actively interfered and got Melissa away from him, she would run back to him the first chance she got. Melissa's reaction left no doubt as to what she would think and do. We would never see her again.

The day before she left on her cruise, I made sure she had packed everything she needed: passport, money, phone, etc. Jack and I offered to drive her to the airport, but she told us Randy would do that. He didn't want her to go on the trip and had had a big argument with her over it, but since it had been paid for, and Melissa wasn't backing down, he had to go along with the plan. Melissa said he didn't speak to her on the way to the airport. She called us when the group arrived in Florida, before boarding the ship, to let us know she had arrived safely.

She told us Randy could not pick her up when she got home, so, of course, we said we'd pick her up.

After the cruise, I had a moment of levity when I spotted Melissa at the curbside of the airport arrival terminal. She was her usual discombobulated self when she had to carry more than two items. She was trying to pull her luggage bag while holding onto her pocketbook, wallet, and a large package, which turned out to be a framed picture of herself on the cruise ship staircase. She kept dropping her belongings. Every time she dropped something, she giggled and laughed with the young woman standing next to her. Her bubbly behavior was what I noticed the most. It had been months since I had seen her that happy. Jack pulled the car up to the curb, and Melissa rushed over. Smiling, she introduced us to a Springboard friend and asked if we could drive her friend home.

They piled into the back seat and started telling us about the trip and all the fun times they had had. They were showing us their pictures when Melissa's cell phone rang. The conversation stopped while she said, "We're driving a friend home…okay…okay…okay, I'll clean it." Poof! You could hear the sadness return to her now-monotone voice and see the smile fade from her face. It was *him*. Randy thought she should be home by then, wanted to know where she was, when she would be home, and wanted her to know what she needed to clean up when she got back. We kept the conversation pleasant while her friend was in the car, but afterward, I attempted to point out to her that Randy should be happy she's back, and not telling her to come home to clean. She again got defensive and upset with me, so I changed the subject. Melissa was sucked right back into this guy's world. Right back into a controlling, toxic relationship. She went home, cleaned, and hid the pictures and mementos of her trip before he got home from work.

We were in a hellish nightmare. Nights were the worst. It wasn't unusual to be awakened by a midnight phone call from Melissa. Randy would have her call us over some outrageous claim or question. One night, he had Melissa call and Jack answered. While he was talking to Melissa, Randy took the phone away from her and told Jack, "You know she hates you." It was like a sport for him. He knew it would make us crazy. But even worse, the phone calls made it almost impossible to get back to sleep. Countless mornings I'd get up and shut off the alarm clock before it even went off—-never having gone to sleep. At work, coffee became my afternoon drug. I was terrified I would fall asleep on the long drive home, since I had caught myself drifting into another lane one night. It was taking a toll on us. All our attempts to break through to Melissa had been fruitless.

Jack suffered the most. There had been a special bond between him and Melissa since the very first time he had picked her up. It was unbearable for him to see her so isolated, controlled, bullied, and God knows what else…Melissa was an adult, thirty-three years old, and there was nothing we could legally do to stop her from seeing this guy or even worse, marrying him. He was a smooth talker who took advantage of Melissa's kindness and her inability to reason with someone who was her superior in intellect. We were trying to buy time, because looming behind every thought or decision we made was the abject fear of losing Melissa to this calculating, scary lout.

Jack had called Melissa one afternoon to check in with her, hoping she'd answer her phone. Of course, Randy was still there. They were both irritated with Jack. Jack was fed up, but so was Randy. He told Jack, "We're moving out." Jack called me at work. "You better come home. They're talking about moving out, and it sounds serious this time: like they've decided."

I could hear Jack's raised voice before I opened the door to our condo unit. Entering the kitchen from the hall, the first person I saw was Melissa. She was sitting on a stool at the kitchen counter. Her face was red, her eyes were watery, her hands were wiping the tears beneath her eyes away, and her bottom lip was trembling. Her shoulders were sloping, and her body sagged on the stool. Sitting next to her was Randy. He was calm and sitting ramrod straight with his hands folded on top of the counter. All he needed was some popcorn to enjoy the show. Jack was standing on the other side of the island with his back to the cooktop and sink, facing them. He was yelling, "…and what about her job? What about her doctors?" He was wringing a dish towel in his hands. His mouth clamped down, his lips formed a pencil-thin line, and his jaw flexed, waiting for a response.

Randy started calmly explaining that he wasn't staying at Melissa's. He said something like, "Melissa, isn't that right?" Even though I hadn't been part of the previous conversation about moving away, this last comment unleashed a fury in me. It brought to the surface all the thoughts and emotions I had tried to tamp down in front of him and Melissa for almost seven months. I couldn't suppress them anymore. All the deception, arrogance, worry, fears, and lying we had endured. It was visceral. And that's when I lost it. I was not going to let him tell Melissa to lie to us. No, no, no! My daughter will not lie to us for him!

We had proof that he was lying because of his parking inability. He thought if he parked on the street behind Melissa's building, we wouldn't notice. He parked his car at such an angle that you could tell it hadn't been moved for several days. The minute he started giving us his story, I jumped in and yelled, "You're lying!" Every time he opened his mouth with another explanation of why he wasn't staying at Melissa's, I yelled, "Liar!" Jack let him have a piece of his mind too. So, there we were, yelling and screaming, with Melissa crying, and Jack throwing paper towel wads against the wall, and then…with that weird semi-smile that revealed his upper front teeth, the guy calmly waited for us to stop ranting, and in a mock contrition-like manner, he stunningly admitted once again that he had been lying to us about everything. I watched him in horror. Maybe it was my nursing experience, or perhaps the abnormal psychology course, but I thought what I was looking at was a learned behavior to control an inner rage. Melissa and Randy went back to her apartment. Apparently, he really didn't have any immediate plans; it had just been another confrontation that he seemed to enjoy immensely.

Two days later, my office phone rang.

"She's gone. He took her."

"What?"

Jack was calling. His voice sounded strange, distant, emotionally flat, like he hardly had the energy to get the words out.

"He took her…I almost hit him…she called the police… It's a long story. There's nothing more I can do. I give up."

"Okay, I'm coming home, but first tell me what happened."

I sat there in my office, momentarily stunned. I finally got up, shut the door, and called Erin in Florida.

Risky Business

"We've lost Melissa, Erin. Her boyfriend took her, and she's not coming back." Erin wanted to know the whole story. I explained there had been a telephone call the night before, and Randy saying, "I'm taking her." "But he didn't take her last night," I said. "Jack went over to her apartment today to see if she was there. It was about one o'clock in the afternoon, and Melissa answered the door in a skimpy, black negligee, and behind her, right as you walk in, was the guy in his underwear, sitting up in the sagging pull-out sleeper-couch. The place was a pigsty. There were clothes all over the floor, dirty dishes, empty food containers, and leftover trash on the floor all around the sofa bed. Jack said he was furious. He looked at Melissa and growled, 'Get dressed!' and then he looked at Randy and yelled, 'And you…get out! I want you out!' He just sat there and said, 'No. Melissa said I could live here.' Jack yelled back, 'Well, I own this place, and you have to get out now, goddammit!' Randy kept saying he wasn't leaving. Jack told me he got so furious, he pushed him back down on the bed and raised his fist like he would hit him. He said, 'I wanted to scare him and get a reaction out of the son-of-a-bitch, but he just laid there with his head on the pillow, looking at me unfazed. It was like he was daring me to hit him.'"

Erin just listened and let me tell her the whole rotten story. I continued. "Melissa had never seen Jack this angry, and Jack said he could hear her in the background crying, 'Leave him alone, or I'll call the cops.' Erin, she called the police! She told them, 'My father's going to beat up my boyfriend.' Jack said he was seething and disgusted and told Randy to get dressed. Two officers came; one talked to Jack, and the other took Randy aside to hear his side of the argument. The officer came over to Jack and said, 'Who owns the apartment?' When Jack said, 'I do,' the cop turned to Randy and told him he had to leave. Randy said, 'Melissa, grab your stuff and let's get out of here.' The officers waited while she got her things together. But Erin, this is the worst part; when Melissa walked out of the apartment, Jack pleaded with her, 'Melissa, I'm your father! Are you going to just walk away from your family?' She just said 'yeah,' and never turned around, Erin. Jack walked home and called me. He's broken.

That's it, Erin, the whole ugly story. What we feared most has happened, and anything we do now will be rejected by Melissa. It's out of our hands."

Erin paused for quite a while. "Listen," she said. "You go home to Jack. I have an idea. It has about a ten percent chance of working. I'm calling Jules." (Julie, or Jules, as we called her, was Erin's best friend from high school and she had known Melissa since she was little.)

It was risky, but Erin and Jules hatched a plan: Erin called me that night and told me Jules had called Melissa pretending she knew nothing. She said Melissa started sobbing and couldn't explain why she was so upset. Jules asked her where she was, and Melissa told her Randy had taken her to his parents' house, which is where I thought he might take her. But as soon as Erin told me that, I had another horrible thought. I only knew where his parents lived, and if he took her anywhere else and took her phone away, as he had done in the past, we might never find her.

Jules got Melissa to agree to breakfast with her the next morning for some "girl talk," but late that night, Melissa, scared and lonely, called her back. Randy had come home from work while Melissa was on the phone and demanded to know who she was talking to. Melissa told him she was talking to an old friend who was taking her out for breakfast in the morning. Jules told Erin she could hear him say, "Oh really?" Randy grabbed the phone out of her hand and told Jules, "You're not picking her up tomorrow. I'm coming to breakfast, I'm driving Melissa, I'm picking the place, and I'm doing the talking because Melissa is handicapped."

Jules called me the next day, and I could tell from her agitated tone that she was seething. "Kathy, they were there waiting for me at the breakfast spot. Melissa was sitting in the corner of the booth, and before I could say anything, this guy says, 'Melissa is handicapped, so I'm doing all the talking for her.' I was pissed, and Melissa started crying. I let him talk. He kept using the word 'handicapped' over and over. I wanted to say, Listen, you f'ing bastard…but instead I said, 'I've known Melissa practically her whole life, and her family never called her handicapped. Melissa is perfectly capable of talking. Aren't you, Melissa?' And she said, 'Yes I am!' Kathy, I recognized his type as soon as he opened his mouth."

Jules's plan was to continue to play dumb and make him feel she was an old friend just having breakfast with Melissa. She turned to Melissa and said, "Melissa, you seem so stressed. Wouldn't it be nice to spend some time with me while your boyfriend looks for an apartment?" She caught him off guard. Melissa nodded. Jules had to get Melissa to agree with the plan, even if she didn't know all the details. Erin called me at work later that afternoon to update me.

"I just talked to Melissa. I asked her if she trusted me and wanted me to help her. Melissa said 'yes,' so I told her, listen, Jules is in her car with her two little kids at the end of the street right now. When Jules calls you, grab your phone, pocketbook, and leave everything else. Get out of the house and get in the car. Promise me you'll do that? Promise? Jules is going to call us, Kathy, as soon as she gets Melissa, and everyone is safe."

I started to thank Erin, but she interrupted me. "It's not over yet, but so far, so good."

I tried to focus on work while I waited for Jules to call. I called Jack and told him what was happening. Maybe, just maybe, this would work. I waited another fifteen minutes but still no call from Jules. I called Erin; she hadn't heard anything either. I couldn't think or concentrate on anything. I grabbed my cell phone and briefcase and left for home. The last leg of my commute involved driving under part of the city through a three-mile tunnel that at the time had no cell phone reception. As I entered the underpass, my cell phone was still silent, but I suddenly felt myself becoming light-headed. Breathe, just breathe. Deep breaths. I must have been holding my breath before that. I was terrified. Please God, please. Let me make it through this tunnel before the phone rings.

I ran into the apartment. "Has Jules called!"

Nothing.

"It's been almost an hour. She should have called by now. This is taking way too long. What's happened?"

Jules had managed to get Melissa, but she had stopped at Burger King so her toddler could use the bathroom, and when they returned to the car, she spotted Melissa on her cell phone. Melissa was talking to Randy, and she had told him where she was. She told Jules that Randy had left work and was on his way to get her. Jules called Erin in a panic.

"What should I do?"

Erin snapped into action. "Jules, give your phone to her right now, and let me talk to her." Jules was incensed. There was no way this guy was going to find them, she thought. Erin talked to Melissa while Jules drove. "I want to see you, Melissa. Lexi wants to see you. If he finds you, he's not going to let you see us. Do you trust me? If you do, then shut your cell phone off right now. Promise? Please, Melissa! I'm going to stay on this phone until you turn your phone off."

Jules took a circuitous route into New Hampshire and stopped at McDonald's for dinner and then drove back to Massachusetts, taking back roads to avoid the highways. It had been three hours since she had picked up Melissa, and Jules wanted to make sure of one last item; she wanted to make sure her husband was home from work.

He was a police officer.

Jack made the last arrangements later that evening. Early the next morning, Jules drove to the Manchester, New Hampshire airport and put Melissa on an 8:00 a.m. flight to Florida. Erin and my sister were waiting at the terminal.

We called the boys after Melissa's flight landed to fill them in on what had just happened. For Jack and me, the situation had been too emotional and too complicated to involve them in the minute-by-minute, hour-by-hour drama of the past day and a half. Besides, we knew neither one of them could do anything—Melissa didn't trust them either.

Knowing Melissa was safe in Florida empowered Jack and me to confront the problem for what we thought it was. But first, we needed to be sure, since we got the impression that the boys thought the flight to Florida was a little over the top.

We called The National Domestic Abuse Hotline. At the time they had a checklist of probably ten to fifteen things listed on their website that a domestic abuser does. Randy did *every* one of them. So, we weren't overreacting. We weren't micro-managing. *He* was the problem. The person we spoke to said it takes an average of seven attempts by the victim before they are able to get away entirely from their abuser, and just the sound of the abuser's voice is enough to bring a victim back. She told us an abuser who was doing all the items on the red flag list would probably escalate to physical violence once their victim is isolated. But we could say out loud now what we couldn't all those prior months: Melissa was a victim of domestic abuse. We were armed, and the situation was serious.

For two months a therapist in Florida worked with Melissa to help her understand the difference between a good relationship and a bad one, and to recognize the danger signs. Melissa's cognitive deficits made analyzing complicated problems difficult. Without guidance, she had a hard time seeing a problem from a forward or backward perspective. She lived mostly in the moment.

Then all hell broke loose.

"We Might Lose Her"

It was midnight, Erin was in bed, and she thought she heard Melissa's cell phone ring. She got up and listened at the door to Melissa's bedroom. Randy had called Melissa, and Erin heard her say she didn't know how much money she had in her bank account. Erin was able to piece enough of the conversation together to realize that Randy was planning to come to Florida to get her, and that Melissa had given him the address. Erin burst into the room, grabbed the phone out of Melissa's hand, and threw it across the room. "How could you tell him where we live! How could you put everyone in danger," she screamed. "How could you!" Erin confiscated the phone and battery. Melissa was in shock. Just as she was with Jack, Melissa had never seen her cousin so angry. In fact, Erin had never gotten angry with Melissa. Ever. Erin shouted, "That does it. I'm going with you to your therapy session tomorrow and you're gonna give me permission to talk to your therapist! Do you understand?"

The therapist called us that afternoon. "I don't think the therapy is working; we might lose her." We had spent eight agonizing months fearing the loss of Melissa. Denial, anger, bargaining, and depression: we had experienced them all. Each stage had taken us deeper and deeper into that vortex of hell.

All my tears had not extinguished the flame of domination that had melted our strong, vibrant daughter into a newly molded stranger.

Sadly, Melissa's story is no different from countless other young girls and women caught up in dangerous, destructive, and lethal relationships. But the difference with Melissa was that although her cognitive disabilities made her easy prey, they also gave our family a fighting chance to get her back.

Jack and I flew down the next day to meet with the therapist. At my sister's, Erin gave us an update. "I think I have a little bit of good news," she said. "Melissa was so shocked when I screamed at her, that I think she might be realizing that Randy isn't good for her. That doesn't mean she won't go back to him though." The seriousness of the situation was finally sinking in. It wasn't just Mom and Dad now trying to get through to her.

As Jules later told us, "Melissa didn't know what to do or think." Melissa wanted to be with friends, family, people—she thrived on social interactions, and as strong as that desire was, she also was under the control of Randy. The two were incompatible. All her actions had had to meet with his approval.

After three weeks, Melissa was still processing what had happened to her and was starting to articulate what she wanted in a girlfriend-boyfriend relationship. Her therapist thought it was time for her to write a letter to Randy to end the relationship and put closure to the whole ordeal. Jack suggested that Melissa mail us the letter and then he would mail it from Boston. We needed to know if Randy was going to come looking for her, and a Boston postmark would indicate to him that she had come home. In the meantime, Jack and I were trying to make sure that Melissa would be safe when she returned. We alerted the whole neighborhood to be on the lookout for the guy. Melissa's neighbors in her building, the many friends in our building, the little grocery down the street, the meter maid, our mailman, the barber, the bank manager, the management company of Melissa's condo building, the dry cleaner, our building's concierge—everyone who knew her.

They all agreed to let us know if they spotted him. We felt that being silent only allows abusers to continue their abuse. We wanted Randy to know that if he showed up, the whole neighborhood would be watching out for Melissa. Three days after Jack mailed Melissa's letter, the building management company for Melissa's condo called and told Jack that Randy had come into their office looking for Melissa. Then Melissa's supervisor at the cinema called to tell us Randy had been there too.

We didn't have any guarantee that Randy wouldn't come back again, or if Melissa would try to contact him, but it was important that she try to regain the independent life she had before she met him. Melissa came home shortly after the last sighting of Randy and reconnected with her friends, joined Springboard again, and blocked Randy from her Facebook page. (Matt agreed to monitor it.) But there was always that uneasy, horrible feeling of not knowing how Melissa would react if she saw or heard from him again.

There were no signs of Randy all fall, then Melissa forwarded an email she received on Jan 2, 2010. "Hey dad I got this e-mail from Randy at 12:53 this morning thought u and mom would like to read it." Randy had written a long, rambling, angry email full of lies and accusations. When we talked about it later that day, Melissa smiled and said, "Yeah, right." She knew it was all hooey. His email only reminded her of how miserable her life had been with him. She could now see his actions for what they were—pathetic attempts to shame and lure her back. She was righteously dismissive of him. We all ignored the letter and Jack and I breathed easier for the first time in over a year.

Melissa had come home. She was thirty-three years old that August, and just emerging from her "teenage years." She didn't see us as parents setting rules anymore, but as confidants and supporters. Watching Jack's anger and him almost hitting the "boyfriend" had been so traumatic that she had no memory of calling the police on Jack. Absolutely none. The situation with this guy had been beyond bad, and Melissa finally understood that.

Getting To Know You

Only 15 percent of individuals with intellectual disabilities are employed, and one in three of them lives in poverty. Melissa had been home for almost six months and her job at the cinema was going well. Then one night that winter, when we picked her up, she cheerfully told us the regional manager was at the cinema and had interviewed her and the rest of the staff. We asked her how it went. "Fine," she said. We could tell by her smile and quick responses that Melissa was pleased with the interview.

"She asked me what jobs I did."

Jack and I felt uneasy. New supervisors or managers always got us nervous. So, we played our "Twenty Questions" game with Melissa to understand what was going on, without dashing her chipper reaction.

"So, what did you tell her?"

"I told her I collected tickets and greeted the people."

"What did she say then?"

"She wanted to know why I didn't work behind the counter and use the registers, so I told her, and she wanted to know why I was away for three months."

"What did she say then?"

"She said, 'Interesting.'"

Judging from the inflection in Melissa's voice when she said "interesting," Melissa thought this was a good thing—her job was *interesting* to the manager. Melissa saw the regional manager as someone who was genuinely interested in her and her work. Jack and I knew better. Another four weeks went by and yet again, Melissa came home and told us she had lost her job.

"Why?" we asked.

"I was late," she said.

"Melissa, were you late three times?"

She put her head down and said, "Yes."

Jack said, "Well, that's the rule, Melissa. You can't be late more than three times."

"I know," she replied.

Melissa understood the attendance policy. We didn't get angry. We had all been through too much. Jack and I were getting tired as well. I was sixty-two and would be retiring in three years, and Jack was sixty-four. Later that week, Jack called Howie to ask about Melissa's firing. Howie brought up the late three times rule and said he had had to abide by the policy. Jack told him he understood. When I got home from work that night, Jack said, "You know, I got the impression Howie felt bad about it." It was years later when Melissa finally opened up about her job at the cinema. She said Randy had deliberately made her late for work twice.

I'm not sure if it's related, but there was a young man whom I'll call Trey, who had physical disabilities and who worked at the cinema with Melissa. He was about five foot four, Black, and used two aluminum forearm crutches to get around. You could hear the metallic ping, ping sound of his crutches as he methodically made his way around the cinema, dragging one foot along as he went. His job was to sweep the lobby and theater aisles after each movie, which he did using the kind of small broom and dustpan with a long handle that many ushers use in theaters. He could hold the dustpan handle and brush up any litter by resting on the forearm part of his crutches.

One night, we saw him making his way down the street past our car as we waited for Melissa. It was a rainy and chilly night, so we offered him a ride home. He told us he lived with his grandmother, who lived about a quarter mile away from the theater. Melissa's commute was complicated, but this fellow's walk was one arduous, slow crawl. It must have taken him a good forty-five minutes to walk to work, and that's assuming no snow or sleet.

Melissa ran into him the following spring in Harvard Square in Cambridge. She was with a friend who had initially recoiled when Melissa first approached him. Her friend tugged her sleeve, and in a hushed voice said, "Melissa, why are you talking to that homeless man?"

Melissa explained, "He's not homeless, he's my friend. I used to work with him." Trey was wearing a backpack (the only way he could carry anything), and Melissa said his clothes looked a little wrinkled. When she told him she had lost her job, he told her he didn't work at the cinema any longer either. He didn't mention why. Maybe he *was* homeless. Maybe his grandmother passed away. Maybe he had another job. Who knows? But Melissa's story hit a nerve in me. I couldn't get it out of my head. Later that night, as Jack and I were getting into bed, I said, "You know, I keep thinking about Trey. Every time a person with disabilities loses a job, or never gets a job, society misses out on an opportunity to interact and learn something. What might we learn, just by smiling and saying 'Hello?'"

It was late, so Jack nodded in agreement. He knew me well enough to let me roll with my thoughts. "We're afraid of our differences. You know? It's so easy to exclude people who look and act differently. It's the same issue Matthew struggles with, and sometimes even Jason. But it's the differences that make life interesting. Right? Jack? Jack?"

Jack was already asleep, but I knew he agreed anyhow.

A new gym had opened on the street behind Melissa's condo building. We got a family membership, and Melissa could use the gym if she wanted—and the pool. After fourteen months of looking for a job and going to the gym to fill up the day, Melissa had gained a group of acquaintances and friends at the gym—more from gabbing and hanging around the front desk than actually working out. I said to her one day, "Screw it, Melissa. Everyone knows you at the gym, why don't you ask them for a job application?" She got the job—part-time front desk attendant. It was a small position to be sure, but to Melissa, having responsibilities made her feel important again. It gave her a sense of purpose, and the best part was that the job gave her an opportunity to be around people, to be a part of a community—her community—her neighborhood. I'm pretty sure Melissa got the job at the gym because they knew her.

Chrysalis

One warm, sunny Saturday in the spring of 2010, Jack and I were taking a stroll through a charming historic neighborhood in Cambridge. The lilac bushes were in bloom, giving off their distinctive scent, and the trees had unfolded their leaves, creating a dappled sunlight effect on the sidewalk. The grass was the greenest it would be all spring and summer, and we were soaking up as much of the day as we could. We had waited all winter for this day to come, and to borrow a line from Robert Browning, it was a "God's in His heaven—All's right with the world!" kind of day. As we walked past a small, white, classical-style New England church, I noticed a banner announcing a book signing event that week for an actress who had become a social advocate and was speaking about her humanitarian experiences in Darfur. She was raising awareness about the project. I stopped short. This was the person who had adopted the little boy in Korea—Misha! This woman was Misha's adoptive mother, Mia Farrow.

I couldn't attend the event (I had a conference in Minnesota that week) so I said, "Jack, you just have to take Melissa to meet her." He prepared a packet with two pictures of Melissa and Misha in the Korean foster home of the Gateleys', along with

Melissa's contact information if they had the opportunity to talk with Mia Farrow. Melissa called me midweek, all excited. "She remembered me, Mom! She remembered my burns!" Jack got on the phone and told me how he had introduced Melissa to Mia Farrow. He said, "Ms. Farrow, I want to introduce my daughter, Doo Hee. She was in the foster home with your son, Misha."

Jack said Ms. Farrow stopped signing her book and sat back for a moment looking at Melissa, and then said, "Are you the little girl with the burns?" He said Melissa's face lit up. Ms. Farrow then told Jack, "When Connie Boll (the social worker who had found the two toddlers in the Korean hospital) called me about the two children, I asked her which child would need the most care, and Connie said, 'I think the little boy who has cerebral palsy will.' Then I'll take the little boy," she said. (She had changed Misha's name to Moses shortly after he arrived.) Because the book signing line was getting long, that was the extent of the exchange, but Melissa was thrilled. She had met someone with a connection to her when she was in Korea.

A few months later, as Jack and I were leaving a movie theater, my cell phone buzzed. It was Melissa. "Mom, guess who just called me!" Not waiting for a response, she said, "Moses, and he's coming up to visit me! He lives in Connecticut."

Jack and Melissa were excited about meeting Moses, but I was apprehensive. They were outgoing individuals, whereas I was more insecure and always nervous about hosting visitors. The irony of the situation was that my unease was always about the lead-up to the event, but once the invited person or persons arrived, I became thoroughly engaged. Jack was the counterweight in our conversations, and I relied on him to be his usual loquacious self. I was also terrible at small talk and dreaded those moments of silence with newfound guests when Jack left the room. So, it was a relief to know that Jack would do the hosting for Moses's visit.

When Moses arrived, Melissa brought him straight over to our apartment to meet Jack. Jack couldn't wait to tell me all about Moses's visit when I got home from work that night.

"We had a nice long lunch. I don't think we left the restaurant until two or two thirty."

"What did you talk about?"

"Most of the conversation we had was telling him about Melissa's life and our family."

"What about Moses? What was he like?"

"He's a nice guy. He seems a little shy and quiet, and I guess you'd say he's slight of build. He lives in Connecticut and is a therapist."

Jack laughed and then said, "I got carried away and started waving my hands around like I usually do when I'm excited, and my voice must have been rising as Melissa actually shushed me in the restaurant." He told me this with a sparkle in his eyes. I knew something funny must have happened. He said the conversation had turned to the choice Moses's adoptive mother had made to adopt him rather than Melissa, and it occurred to Jack that Moses was our "almost" son. That was all Jack needed: He loved to joke and tease Melissa, or any other poor victim around him, so from that moment on, Moses was our "almost" son. An unfeigned comfort level had developed between the three of them. Jack said Moses had a speaking engagement at an area college at the end of the month and would visit again.

This time I would get to meet him.

For his return visit, we invited Moses for dinner on our patio; after his second helping of rice, we noticed he loved rice as much as Jason and Melissa—one more thing Jack could tease him about. During his visit, I could see that Moses had a very slight limp and footdrop in one leg, and that he favored one hand over the other, weaker one; these were the main physical markers of his cerebral palsy. After dinner, our conversation moved from the table to the cushioned patio furniture, and we all talked long into the evening. One moment that touched my heart was when Moses paused, turned to Melissa, and said something to the effect of, "Melissa, our childhoods were similar because I had operations too. It's another thing we have in common." Forgetting Melissa during a conversation was easy to do. She could agree or disagree with what was being discussed, but found it difficult to expound on the subject, so would remain mostly silent. Moses had picked up on this and had made a point to include her in the conversation. He often reflected on what had just been said and would stop to comment on how it related to a broader topic. His introspection impressed me.

Moses told us he was a Licensed Marriage and Family Therapist and would be speaking about interracial and international adoptions the following day at Tufts University. He asked us if he could use parts of Melissa's adoption story in his talk: Melissa had already agreed. Moses talked about some of the research that had been done, showing that children of international and interracial adoptions identified more with the culture of their adoptive families rather than their own racial makeup, and tended to date and marry persons who had their adoptive family's ethnicity. It was a topic that he had been doing a lot of thinking about, but the threads of our broader conversation were around issues of abandonment and identity, and the ripple effects they create for a lot of adoptees. Moses said that he had told some friends about his mother's call and her meeting Jack and Melissa. He said he had been initially reluctant to connect with Melissa, but his friends had urged him to call her. He explained to us that if meeting Melissa had been presented as an option just one year earlier, he didn't think he would have been prepared emotionally to meet her or us. He had still been dealing with his own abandonment issues. I sensed a pain in his voice.

Jack suggested that they both write a letter to Connie Boll, who had found the two all those years ago, letting her know they had connected. Their letter has long been lost, but in Jack's introductory letter to Connie, he wrote:

"…each in their own way, and for their own needs, have been seeking and wondering about their roots. Their friendship is taking on a special meaning. Something only the two of them share."

Walking back to Melissa's apartment after his first visit, Moses said, "Just think, Melissa, we were both found on the streets of Seoul, and here we are, walking the streets of Boston together. We've found each other."

Meeting Moses was a transformative moment for Melissa. Here was someone who looked like her and who shared part of her adoption story. In the beauty and simplicity of Melissa's thinking, this connection had satisfied her search for her Korean family. In her mind, Moses *was* her Korean family. But another transformation had occurred. Melissa had turned a corner. Whether it was because of the counseling she had received in Florida or realizing how much her family and friends cared about her, or her job at the gym, or meeting Mia Farrow and Moses, I don't know. It was probably all of them, but I do know that she asserted a bold confidence in herself and a new level of maturity. The yoke of subjugation and fear that had held her down for those long nine months had finally gone.

Spreading Wings

Melissa's joy in meeting people is pure. Because of this, she knows many individuals in our neighborhood, and, amazingly, she remembers their names and even their pets' names. I think the first inkling of this ability happened before she could even speak, about five months after she arrived. As I remember, it was a Saturday afternoon and I had just walked into my parents' house when I heard Jack call out, "Kathy, come see this! Missy's playing the Memory Game with your mother, and she's winning!" The Memory Game is a game where you have to turn over a picture card and match it with its unturned picture card. There are about twenty to thirty cards to match. I was sure my mother was letting Melissa win the game, so I pulled a chair up to the kitchen table. Mom shuffled the cards, looked at me, and snickered, "Watch this." She laid the cards out on the table in a grid-like fashion. "Okay, Melissa, you go first." Melissa was kneeling on a padded kitchen chair and began flipping over and matching one card after another. She giggled as she amassed a pile of cards on her side. Mom barely got a chance to match anything, and when Melissa won, Mom sat back in her chair, clapped her hands, and said, "She beats me every damn time!" How was she doing this? How does she remember these pictures? I thought.

I still don't know why, or how that part of her brain works so remarkably—while other parts fail her—nevertheless, to witness her interactions with people is a beautiful thing. It's not that she remembers people's names; it's that she cares about them and asks about their family and even their pets. And people reciprocate. For instance, one time Melissa and I were eating at a local restaurant, and she had jumped up from the table to say hello to someone she knew from the gym who had just come in with three business associates. The woman got up from her seat, hugged her, and asked Melissa to introduce her to me, so she could say how much she appreciated Melissa's cheerfulness. Other gym members have told Jack and me similar stories and have told us they look out for her—she's family.

Melissa has become quite the character in our family. She called me one day and told me she was having chest pains. She rattled off all the usual signs and symptoms (she had heard me talk about the warning signs of a heart attack since she was little). Jack and I rushed her to the hospital, which is luckily only three blocks down the street. Not having any family health history to reference, the ER gave her a thorough workup, while Jack and I waited nervously in the waiting room—for hours. She finally emerged through the ER doors, came over to us, and said, "I just pulled a muscle in my chest," and almost simultaneously looked at a fellow sitting near us and said, "Hi, Phil, what are you doing here? How's your wife?" He told her his wife was in the hospital receiving treatment. "Thanks for asking, Melissa." She then introduced us to Phil. Jack got up to get the car in the parking garage, but Melissa said, "No, I'm going to walk home. I don't want to miss the condo meeting, it stared at seven o'clock, and I can get home faster if I walk."

And off she went. Jack and I laughed. Never one to miss an opportunity to be around people, Melissa was determined to get home and see her neighbors even if she understood diddly squat about any of the financial details in the meeting.

A few summers ago, Melissa and her girlfriend took the ferry to visit Matthew for a weekend in Provincetown, Cape Cod (a seaside vacation town and destination for many of our neighbors and members of Melissa's gym). Jack and I were at the pier waiting for the ferry to arrive Sunday evening when Matthew called. "Mom, Dad, I had to call and tell you this before Melissa's ferry gets in: Melissa had a blast! She was the *Queen* of P-Town. She knows everyone!" When we met them at the ferry dock, her girlfriend shook her head and laughed. "Oh my God, what a weekend! Melissa knows everyone down there. It took us forever to walk to the restaurant last night. She kept bumping into people she knew."

A butterfly—that's how I think of Melissa. Most people who come upon one will stop to watch it flutter. The encounter usually leaves them smiling. That's how I see her. She leaves people smiling.

Epilogue

Bountiful

When I was younger, I thought that if I planted a McIntosh seed, it would grow into a McIntosh tree, and if I planted a Gravenstein seed, it would grow into a Gravenstein tree. But let's say you eat a Baldwin apple and decide to plant all the seeds in that one apple, and they all sprout. Every seed will produce a tree, but none of them will be a Baldwin. That's because, just like humans, apple trees are products of sexual fertilization and reproduction, and every seed in an apple has a unique set of genes—which is why we're not clones of our parents, and we have our own distinct set of genes.

Matthew's sexual orientation and Jason's ADHD are innate—part of their makeup and core parts of who they are. It just is who they are—the same goes for Melissa's affable personality. Even buried under the trauma and neglect of her early childhood, when she was wasting away in the children's hospital in Seoul, Melissa's personality was there. When she had been unable to speak, she had used the only thing she could—her eyes, to pull those who had the patience to look closer and "hear" her eyes' silent eloquence entreating a human connection.

And despite the botany lesson Luther gave Dad and me, it remained a mystery why our abundant apple trees never produced any seedlings. I've since learned that growing apple trees from seed is difficult: if you can coax one to sprout, and you have the patience, it can take up to six or eight years to produce fruit and to even know what variety you're growing. Because of this, most apple trees are grown from root stock—basically an apple tree sapling with a healthy root system and stem that has been cut and from which a branch of another apple variety could be grafted onto. The selected graft—the variety of apple you want to grow—becomes the part of the tree that produces the desired fruit.

When early European settlers brought apple seeds with them to the New World, many different varieties of apple were grown. Most were bitter and used for cider making, yet occasionally, a farmer would discover a tree that was different. The tree was like all the other trees, but its fruit was different. If the farmer took the time to discover the unique qualities of the fruit, whether it be the sweetness or hardiness, etc., the tree was not disregarded, it was cultivated and nourished, and, much like humankind, this small link in the chain of plant biodiversity resulted in a species made stronger and richer.

Stopping by farmstands scattered along rural back roads of New England is one of my favorite things to do in the warm, waning days of summer and early days of fall. Writing this now, I can close my eyes and hear the crunch of gravel under the car tires as we pull off the road to stop. Opening the car door, the rush of warm air envelops my face, and I can hear a chorus of cicadas heralding the end of summer. The grasses along the edges of the parking area are coated with the dust of summer, and the rich, earthy smells of soil and harvested hay greet me. The farmstand is awash in color—sunflowers, tomatoes, squash, corn, peaches, pears, and apples. And I can see honeybees languidly circling and landing on the ripe, sun-warmed produce. In the distance, there might even be a well-tended apple orchard.

Sometimes when we take these little country road trips, we come upon a sign pointing to a path or trail and we stop to explore. And there, in an open, sunny section of the trail, we sometimes chance upon it. It might be behind a piece of rotting fence, a crumbling stone wall, or maybe in an overgrown field next to the path. But there it is—an old, forgotten apple tree—the cidery scent of its fallen fruit urging us to sample its sweet bounty. But who does this fruit belong to? Who planted this tree? Was it planted long ago by a farmer to provide nourishment for his family? Still, the old tree continues to share its gifts. But, for who? Us? The birds? The field critters? The bees? The earth, from which it grew? Who benefits?

All do
And we give thanks.

About the Author

Kathleen Tumminello is a retired Occupational Health Nurse who lives in Boston, Ma with her husband Jack.

Made in United States
North Haven, CT
09 February 2024

48547333R00119